# The Record Book

Sherry K. Hayes

Copyright © 2018 by Large Family Mothering
All rights reserved.

ISBN-13: 978-1981524334
ISBN-10: 1981524339

Visit: momdelights.com

# Table of Contents

| Page | Title |
|---|---|
| 1-4 | Introduction |
| 5-12 | How To Use This Book |

# Table of Contents

| Page | Title |
|---|---|
|  |  |

# Introduction

Homeschooling is a terrific way to grow your children and your family. It is also a great way to get you feeling overwhelmed and unable to keep on top of it all.

First, there is the planning. So many choices! Then there is the scheduling; will you go by the conventional school year or will you go the year-round route? Then there are the logistics; should you do book work or fold the laundry first thing in the morning?

Finally, there is what you actually accomplish every day. Some of it is in a tangible form, such as pages of books read or filled in.

But then there are all of the other learning moments, such as when you are folding clothes together (we call them "clothes folding parties") and you start talking about the events leading up to the Civil War.

Or what about grocery shopping and exploring the different types of bread or where certain cheeses originated from and then hurrying home to look the countries up on a map and watch videos of making bread and cheese on YouTube, and on and on.

How can you keep track of all of this "educating" you are doing together?

This is what I wondered a few years back. In my household was every age and stage of childhood, from newborn infant to college-aged young person. There was always so much going on, so much that needed to be recorded, but I was at a loss as to how to capture it in a way was both simple and thorough.

Then, while visiting my husband in his office one day, I got out a ruler, a legal notepad, and a black magic marker and began to sketch out a form I could use to keep track of what we were accomplishing together.

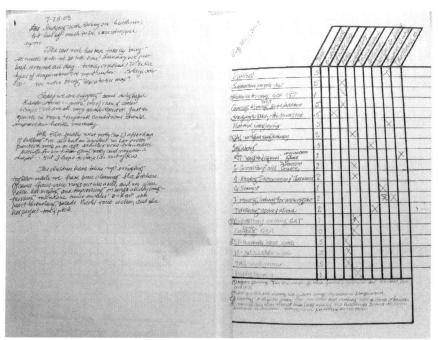

I decided to have a column to name the activity and the initials of the children participating, a place to record the time spent, and then a number of columns named with the academic areas covered by the activity, such as:

- Bible and life skills
- Language arts
- World Studies (including what is generally called "social studies," but I hate the name)
- Math

- Science
- Physical activity and outings
- Handicraft

The end result wasn't polished or pretty, but it was practical and useful. After making multiple copies

I three-hole punched them and placed them in a bracketed folder. This "record book" was then easy to carry around and make notations wherever I went, a great convenience for a mom who was usually chasing down toddlers and nursing babies all over the house.

Since I found them so helpful and since I knew they could help other moms like me, I created a digital form of these pages and offered them as a free PDF download on my blog,

MomDelights.com. (You can find them on the Freebies Page at the top menu.)

However, I realized this was not enough. A lot of ladies were going to download the free PDF and get distracted (as I always do) while the file sat gathering digital dust on their hard drives.

What to do?—create a physical copy of this resource, already copied and bound, so that moms could order it and use it as soon as it arrived in the mail!

And here you have it—all pretty and filled with bonus materials that I hope will bless your homeschooling flip-flops off!

# How to Use This Book

**The Record Book** is not meant to be a homeschool planner. These pages are for keeping track of all of the learning that is already happening so you will:

• have a record for authorities

• be able to accurately produce high school transcripts

• have a bank of memories both for sentimental and practical use later on.

Each page incudes places to write down the activity, the time spent, the children who were involved, and the education area(s) covered. There is also a place for notes, such as the attitude of the children, the circumstances of the day, or even some directions for the next day.

**Here is an actual example of what this would look like:**

Yesterday we held a history movie marathon. We watched *War and Peace* and *Genghis Khan* (the 1950's versions), only stopping to eat. While enjoying some hot dogs and fries, we discussed the different time periods of the movies, the settings, the people, etc. During dinner Daddy had the kids go up to the map in our dining room and find the different places featured in the movies we were watching.

This morning I am recording all of this as genuine learning experiences and giving credit in the areas of "world history," "geography," "social studies," and "language arts."

**Another instance** would be when a child sits down with a bin of Legos and creates and plays for hours. You KNOW there is oodles of learning that should count somehow, and *The Record Book* is just the thing to make sure it does. Lego time (along with almost every other sort of free-play) fits right in with STEAM (Science, Technology, Engineering, Arts, and Math) because a child is involving himself with these "educational" areas:

- Logic
- Spatial relationships
- Sequencing
- Physics
- Applied mathematical reasoning

So I would make sure and write down such play time and put a check below these boxes:

- Science
- Art
- Math

In fact, when we start thinking through all the activities interactions we have with our children each day, legitimate learning of one sort or another is going on pretty much every minute they are not asleep!

**The Record Book** is all about capturing all of that learning and putting it down on paper so that we will have a record.

We have filled in these categories for you on the following pages. They are:

**Bible and Life.** This category includes anything about the Bible, such as devotions in the morning, copywork, reading aloud, church, listening to good teaching online, etc.

For the "life" category, there are many possibilities; such as spontaneous talks about the meaning of life, character, work ethic (doing chores), giving to others (when your kids help out Gramma or any other elderly person, or babysit their own siblings or other children), handling your emotions, finding your way through life, etc.

**Language Arts.** Of course this will include reading and grammar, but also anything that causes your children to use language, such as understanding a good, old movie with lots of dialogue, or watching a foreign film with subtitles. And don't forget discussion times, this is actually where a great amount of language arts has its roots. (Oh, and Bible and Life counts for this, too.)

**Math.** At first blush this category seems confined to only a few types of activities. However, kids learn this subject best by application, so activities such as counting their change so they can go to the dollar store, then going to the dollar store and calculating how many items they can purchase, then calculating the tax on those items (if your state charges any), then paying for those items themselves, can all "count" as math. Also, there are many handicrafts that use mathematical reasoning, such as knitting, quilting, etc. Certain play activities involve math, such as Legos, magnetic sets, board games, and the like. You could even count decluttering and super cleaning your house as math, since a lot of sorting, discriminating, and spatial relationship thinking is going on (think of rearranging furniture in a room or items in a desk—you didn't know you were a genius at math, did you?). (By the way, there areas of Bible study that have to do with math, such as when you have the kids look up verses, calculating the differences in ages of the patriarchs, numbers of the troops mentioned in the Old Testament, etc.).

**World Studies.** Basically all of what is referred to as "social studies," but with less of the influence of the progressivism of the early 1900's. It's amazing how much more interesting the whole discipline became to us when we began to see it in the light of how God has been working all along to perform His ends. Think here of geography, history, political studies, current events, cultural studies, etc. So much of this can be addressed via Internet videos such as those from Prager U that you hardly need to stress. I strongly suggest you re-educate yourself with a God-centered view of history and the social sciences (see my blog for resources).

**Science.** The essence of this word is "the state of knowing" and this includes everything in the universe, from quantum theory to caring for a turtle in an aquarium.

**Arts and Handicraft.** Fufu arts and crafts may have a small place in a child's life, but we all know cutesy cut-outs are destined for File 13. Instead, why not allow children to create with real things, such as cloth, thread, yarn, and wood? Cake decorating and room decorating could be included here. Or what about party planning, pottery, nail painting, etc.?

**Physical Activities.** Some families like to "sport" together, but there is more. What about hikes, bikes, yardwork, painting a room, dancing, deep cleaning, moving, outside job…

**Outings/Life Skills.** This is all the stuff that we think doesn't count, but should count more than all the other stuff. Such as church functions, weddings, parties, theater and orchestral presentations, family reunions, caring for new babies and toddlers, dealing with illness, caring for the elderly, home repairs, personal finances, shopping, buying a bike or car, dating working, starting a small business…

You will also need to develop your own abbreviations for learning activities, such as:

- RA for Reading Aloud
- SR for Self Reading
- F for "flick" or movie

- D for discussion

**If you struggle with feeling legitimate about counting all of these different activities as "school," consider this:**

Just because a child spends 6-8 hours a day away from home does not mean all those hours are actually used for profitable learning. Think about all the time spent riding the bus, standing in line, roll call, assemblies, field trips, discipline issues, boring-awful-politically-correct content, waiting for the teacher to help or explain, shuffling from one class to another, etc.

**What we get to do when we homeschool is two things:**

1. Take the nuggets of true learning and focus in on them.

2. Apply true learning to real life.

These two things are what conventional schooling is absolutely inept at. First of all, the curriculum of public schooling is schizophrenic due to the massive amounts of social engineering attempts from all sides. One side says, "Stick to the basics," the other side says, "Deal with emotional issues," another side says, "Test, test, test," another says, "Make them global citizens," and on and on.

Second of all, when you take kids out of the "real world" and set them in concrete buildings which don't even have windows, you can only pretend to help them apply learning to life. A child can learn how to count change with a worksheet, but he has little chance of actually using that knowledge in a classroom environment. Conventional schooling can teach courses on "getting along," but removing children from their families will keep them from learning the true core of the message.

(Some would argue that this is the goal; to make it look like people are being educated while keeping them from applying what they know, creating a massive, clueless populace easily controlled from the top.)

Having your kids help entertain the babies while you fix dinner is not harming them. In reality you are doing more for your children with that simple "chore" than any school could do with a 20-hour curriculum on "helpers," or "cooperation."

**I hope this is painting a picture in your mind:** I hope you are beginning to see that the hours your children spend in true learning everyday are ***enormous.***

But if you're still unsure, it might be helpful to take a few moments to reexamine the meaning of learning itself.

Here is the 1828 Webster's dictionary definition:

> Gaining knowledge by instruction or reading, by study, by experience or observation; acquiring skill by practice.

Here's something Charlotte Mason said:

> Self-education is the only possible education; the rest is mere veneer laid on the surface of a child's nature.

Here's what God said about the education of Jesus:

> And Jesus increased in wisdom and stature, and in favour with God and man.
> -Luke 2:52

There are also books and websites which offer alternative

ideas to current thought on the subject. Here are a few suggestions:

> *The Successful Homeschool Family Handbook*
>
> By Dr. Raymond and Dorothy Moore
>
> *For the Children's Sake: Foundations of Education for Home and School*
>
> by Susan Schaeffer Macaulay

And don't forget the posts on my blog, MomDelights.com!

After taking some time to consider what learning is for you and your children, you can begin to understand that almost anything and everything you do each day has some educational value.

**Take these pages and record them all in a way that will count.**

# Examples:

# Attendance Rercord For:
_____

**Month:**

| S | M | T | W | Th | F | S |
|---|---|---|---|----|---|---|
|   |   |   |   |    |   |   |
|   |   |   |   |    |   |   |
|   |   |   |   |    |   |   |
|   |   |   |   |    |   |   |
|   |   |   |   |    |   |   |

**Month:**

| S | M | T | W | Th | F | S |
|---|---|---|---|----|---|---|
|   |   |   |   |    |   |   |
|   |   |   |   |    |   |   |
|   |   |   |   |    |   |   |
|   |   |   |   |    |   |   |
|   |   |   |   |    |   |   |

**Month:**

| S | M | T | W | Th | F | S |
|---|---|---|---|----|---|---|
|   |   |   |   |    |   |   |
|   |   |   |   |    |   |   |
|   |   |   |   |    |   |   |
|   |   |   |   |    |   |   |
|   |   |   |   |    |   |   |

**Month:**

| S | M | T | W | Th | F | S |
|---|---|---|---|----|---|---|
|   |   |   |   |    |   |   |
|   |   |   |   |    |   |   |
|   |   |   |   |    |   |   |
|   |   |   |   |    |   |   |
|   |   |   |   |    |   |   |

**Month:**

| S | M | T | W | Th | F | S |
|---|---|---|---|----|---|---|
|   |   |   |   |    |   |   |
|   |   |   |   |    |   |   |
|   |   |   |   |    |   |   |
|   |   |   |   |    |   |   |
|   |   |   |   |    |   |   |

**Month:**

| S | M | T | W | Th | F | S |
|---|---|---|---|----|---|---|
|   |   |   |   |    |   |   |
|   |   |   |   |    |   |   |
|   |   |   |   |    |   |   |
|   |   |   |   |    |   |   |
|   |   |   |   |    |   |   |

Attendance Rercord For:
_____

| Month: | | | | | | |
|---|---|---|---|---|---|---|
| S | M | T | W | Th | F | S |

| Month: | | | | | | |
|---|---|---|---|---|---|---|
| S | M | T | W | Th | F | S |

| Month: | | | | | | |
|---|---|---|---|---|---|---|
| S | M | T | W | Th | F | S |

| Month: | | | | | | |
|---|---|---|---|---|---|---|
| S | M | T | W | Th | F | S |

| Month: | | | | | | |
|---|---|---|---|---|---|---|
| S | M | T | W | Th | F | S |

| Month: | | | | | | |
|---|---|---|---|---|---|---|
| S | M | T | W | Th | F | S |

# Activity

date(s): _____

| | Initials | Time | Bible and Life | Language Arts | Math | World Studies | Science | Arts and Handicraft | Physical Activity | Outings/Life Skill |
|---|---|---|---|---|---|---|---|---|---|---|
| | | | | | | | | | | |
| | | | | | | | | | | |
| | | | | | | | | | | |
| | | | | | | | | | | |
| | | | | | | | | | | |
| | | | | | | | | | | |
| | | | | | | | | | | |
| | | | | | | | | | | |
| | | | | | | | | | | |
| | | | | | | | | | | |
| | | | | | | | | | | |
| | | | | | | | | | | |

Notes:

# Activity

date(s): _____

| | Initials | Time | Bible and Life | Language Arts | Math | World Studies | Science | Arts and Handicraft | Physical Activity | Outings/Life Skill |
|---|---|---|---|---|---|---|---|---|---|---|
| | | | | | | | | | | |
| | | | | | | | | | | |
| | | | | | | | | | | |
| | | | | | | | | | | |
| | | | | | | | | | | |
| | | | | | | | | | | |
| | | | | | | | | | | |
| | | | | | | | | | | |
| | | | | | | | | | | |
| | | | | | | | | | | |
| | | | | | | | | | | |
| | | | | | | | | | | |
| | | | | | | | | | | |

Notes:

# Activity

date(s): _____

| | Initials | Time | Bible and Life | Language Arts | Math | World Studies | Science | Arts and Handicraft | Physical Activity | Outings/Life Skill |
|---|---|---|---|---|---|---|---|---|---|---|
| | | | | | | | | | | |
| | | | | | | | | | | |
| | | | | | | | | | | |
| | | | | | | | | | | |
| | | | | | | | | | | |
| | | | | | | | | | | |
| | | | | | | | | | | |
| | | | | | | | | | | |
| | | | | | | | | | | |
| | | | | | | | | | | |
| | | | | | | | | | | |
| | | | | | | | | | | |
| | | | | | | | | | | |

Notes:

# Activity

date(s): _____

| | Initials | Time | Bible and Life | Language Arts | Math | World Studies | Science | Arts and Handicraft | Physical Activity | Outings/Life Skill |
|---|---|---|---|---|---|---|---|---|---|---|

Notes:

# Activity

date(s): _____

| | Initials | Time | Bible and Life | Language Arts | Math | World Studies | Science | Arts and Handicraft | Physical Activity | Outings/Life Skiill |
|---|---|---|---|---|---|---|---|---|---|---|
| | | | | | | | | | | |
| | | | | | | | | | | |
| | | | | | | | | | | |
| | | | | | | | | | | |
| | | | | | | | | | | |
| | | | | | | | | | | |
| | | | | | | | | | | |
| | | | | | | | | | | |
| | | | | | | | | | | |
| | | | | | | | | | | |
| | | | | | | | | | | |
| | | | | | | | | | | |

Notes:

# Activity

date(s): _____

| | Initials | Time | Bible and Life | Language Arts | Math | World Studies | Science | Arts and Handicraft | Physical Activity | Outings/Life Skill |
|---|---|---|---|---|---|---|---|---|---|---|
| | | | | | | | | | | |
| | | | | | | | | | | |
| | | | | | | | | | | |
| | | | | | | | | | | |
| | | | | | | | | | | |
| | | | | | | | | | | |
| | | | | | | | | | | |
| | | | | | | | | | | |
| | | | | | | | | | | |
| | | | | | | | | | | |
| | | | | | | | | | | |
| | | | | | | | | | | |
| | | | | | | | | | | |

Notes:

# Activity

date(s): _____

| | Initials | Time | Bible and Life | Language Arts | Math | World Studies | Science | Arts and Handicraft | Physical Activity | Outings/Life Skill |
|---|---|---|---|---|---|---|---|---|---|---|
| | | | | | | | | | | |
| | | | | | | | | | | |
| | | | | | | | | | | |
| | | | | | | | | | | |
| | | | | | | | | | | |
| | | | | | | | | | | |
| | | | | | | | | | | |
| | | | | | | | | | | |
| | | | | | | | | | | |
| | | | | | | | | | | |
| | | | | | | | | | | |
| | | | | | | | | | | |
| | | | | | | | | | | |

Notes:

# Activity

date(s): _____

|  | Initials | Time | Bible and Life | Language Arts | Math | World Studies | Science | Arts and Handicraft | Physical Activity | Outings/Life Skill |
|---|---|---|---|---|---|---|---|---|---|---|
| _____ | | | | | | | | | | |
| _____ | | | | | | | | | | |
| _____ | | | | | | | | | | |
| _____ | | | | | | | | | | |
| _____ | | | | | | | | | | |
| _____ | | | | | | | | | | |
| _____ | | | | | | | | | | |
| _____ | | | | | | | | | | |
| _____ | | | | | | | | | | |
| _____ | | | | | | | | | | |
| _____ | | | | | | | | | | |
| _____ | | | | | | | | | | |
| _____ | | | | | | | | | | |

Notes:

# Activity

date(s): _____

| | Initials | Time | Bible and Life | Language Arts | Math | World Studies | Science | Arts and Handicraft | Physical Activity | Outings/Life Skill |
|---|---|---|---|---|---|---|---|---|---|---|
| | | | | | | | | | | |
| | | | | | | | | | | |
| | | | | | | | | | | |
| | | | | | | | | | | |
| | | | | | | | | | | |
| | | | | | | | | | | |
| | | | | | | | | | | |
| | | | | | | | | | | |
| | | | | | | | | | | |
| | | | | | | | | | | |
| | | | | | | | | | | |
| | | | | | | | | | | |
| | | | | | | | | | | |

Notes:

# Activity

date(s): _____

| | Initials | Time | Bible and Life | Language Arts | Math | World Studies | Science | Arts and Handicraft | Physical Activity | Outings/Life Skill |
|---|---|---|---|---|---|---|---|---|---|---|
| | | | | | | | | | | |
| | | | | | | | | | | |
| | | | | | | | | | | |
| | | | | | | | | | | |
| | | | | | | | | | | |
| | | | | | | | | | | |
| | | | | | | | | | | |
| | | | | | | | | | | |
| | | | | | | | | | | |
| | | | | | | | | | | |
| | | | | | | | | | | |
| | | | | | | | | | | |
| | | | | | | | | | | |
| | | | | | | | | | | |

Notes:

## Activity

date(s): _____

| | Initials | Time | Bible and Life | Language Arts | Math | World Studies | Science | Arts and Handicraft | Physical Activity | Outings/Life Skill |
|---|---|---|---|---|---|---|---|---|---|---|
| | | | | | | | | | | |
| | | | | | | | | | | |
| | | | | | | | | | | |
| | | | | | | | | | | |
| | | | | | | | | | | |
| | | | | | | | | | | |
| | | | | | | | | | | |
| | | | | | | | | | | |
| | | | | | | | | | | |
| | | | | | | | | | | |
| | | | | | | | | | | |
| | | | | | | | | | | |
| | | | | | | | | | | |

Notes:

# Activity

date(s): _____

| | Initials | Time | Bible and Life | Language Arts | Math | World Studies | Science | Arts and Handicraft | Physical Activity | Outings/Life Skiill |
|---|---|---|---|---|---|---|---|---|---|---|
| _____ | | | | | | | | | | |
| _____ | | | | | | | | | | |
| _____ | | | | | | | | | | |
| _____ | | | | | | | | | | |
| _____ | | | | | | | | | | |
| _____ | | | | | | | | | | |
| _____ | | | | | | | | | | |
| _____ | | | | | | | | | | |
| _____ | | | | | | | | | | |
| _____ | | | | | | | | | | |
| _____ | | | | | | | | | | |
| _____ | | | | | | | | | | |
| _____ | | | | | | | | | | |

Notes:

# Activity

date(s): _____

|  | Initials | Time | Bible and Life | Language Arts | Math | World Studies | Science | Arts and Handicraft | Physical Activity | Outings/Life Skill |
|---|---|---|---|---|---|---|---|---|---|---|
| _____ | | | | | | | | | | |
| _____ | | | | | | | | | | |
| _____ | | | | | | | | | | |
| _____ | | | | | | | | | | |
| _____ | | | | | | | | | | |
| _____ | | | | | | | | | | |
| _____ | | | | | | | | | | |
| _____ | | | | | | | | | | |
| _____ | | | | | | | | | | |
| _____ | | | | | | | | | | |
| _____ | | | | | | | | | | |
| _____ | | | | | | | | | | |
| _____ | | | | | | | | | | |

Notes:

# Activity

date(s): _____

| | Initials | Time | Bible and Life | Language Arts | Math | World Studies | Science | Arts and Handicraft | Physical Activity | Outings/Life Skill |
|---|---|---|---|---|---|---|---|---|---|---|
| | | | | | | | | | | |
| | | | | | | | | | | |
| | | | | | | | | | | |
| | | | | | | | | | | |
| | | | | | | | | | | |
| | | | | | | | | | | |
| | | | | | | | | | | |
| | | | | | | | | | | |
| | | | | | | | | | | |
| | | | | | | | | | | |
| | | | | | | | | | | |
| | | | | | | | | | | |
| | | | | | | | | | | |

Notes:

# Activity

date(s): _____

| | Initials | Time | Bible and Life | Language Arts | Math | World Studies | Science | Arts and Handicraft | Physical Activity | Outings/Life Skill |
|---|---|---|---|---|---|---|---|---|---|---|
| | | | | | | | | | | |
| | | | | | | | | | | |
| | | | | | | | | | | |
| | | | | | | | | | | |
| | | | | | | | | | | |
| | | | | | | | | | | |
| | | | | | | | | | | |
| | | | | | | | | | | |
| | | | | | | | | | | |
| | | | | | | | | | | |
| | | | | | | | | | | |
| | | | | | | | | | | |

Notes:

## Activity

date(s): _____

| | Initials | Time | Bible and Life | Language Arts | Math | World Studies | Science | Arts and Handicraft | Physical Activity | Outings/Life Skill |
|---|---|---|---|---|---|---|---|---|---|---|
| | | | | | | | | | | |
| | | | | | | | | | | |
| | | | | | | | | | | |
| | | | | | | | | | | |
| | | | | | | | | | | |
| | | | | | | | | | | |
| | | | | | | | | | | |
| | | | | | | | | | | |
| | | | | | | | | | | |
| | | | | | | | | | | |
| | | | | | | | | | | |
| | | | | | | | | | | |
| | | | | | | | | | | |

Notes:

## Activity

date(s): _____

| | Initials | Time | Bible and Life | Language Arts | Math | World Studies | Science | Arts and Handicraft | Physical Activity | Outings/Life Skill |
|---|---|---|---|---|---|---|---|---|---|---|
| | | | | | | | | | | |
| | | | | | | | | | | |
| | | | | | | | | | | |
| | | | | | | | | | | |
| | | | | | | | | | | |
| | | | | | | | | | | |
| | | | | | | | | | | |
| | | | | | | | | | | |
| | | | | | | | | | | |
| | | | | | | | | | | |
| | | | | | | | | | | |
| | | | | | | | | | | |

Notes:

# Activity

date(s): _____

| | Initials | Time | Bible and Life | Language Arts | Math | World Studies | Science | Arts and Handicraft | Physical Activity | Outings/Life Skill |
|---|---|---|---|---|---|---|---|---|---|---|
| | | | | | | | | | | |
| | | | | | | | | | | |
| | | | | | | | | | | |
| | | | | | | | | | | |
| | | | | | | | | | | |
| | | | | | | | | | | |
| | | | | | | | | | | |
| | | | | | | | | | | |
| | | | | | | | | | | |
| | | | | | | | | | | |
| | | | | | | | | | | |
| | | | | | | | | | | |
| | | | | | | | | | | |

Notes:

# Activity

date(s): _____

| | Initials | Time | Bible and Life | Language Arts | Math | World Studies | Science | Arts and Handicraft | Physical Activity | Outings/Life Skiill |
|---|---|---|---|---|---|---|---|---|---|---|
| | | | | | | | | | | |
| | | | | | | | | | | |
| | | | | | | | | | | |
| | | | | | | | | | | |
| | | | | | | | | | | |
| | | | | | | | | | | |
| | | | | | | | | | | |
| | | | | | | | | | | |
| | | | | | | | | | | |
| | | | | | | | | | | |
| | | | | | | | | | | |
| | | | | | | | | | | |
| | | | | | | | | | | |

Notes:

# Activity

date(s): _____

| | Initials | Time | Bible and Life | Language Arts | Math | World Studies | Science | Arts and Handicraft | Physical Activity | Outings/Life Skill |
|---|---|---|---|---|---|---|---|---|---|---|
| | | | | | | | | | | |
| | | | | | | | | | | |
| | | | | | | | | | | |
| | | | | | | | | | | |
| | | | | | | | | | | |
| | | | | | | | | | | |
| | | | | | | | | | | |
| | | | | | | | | | | |
| | | | | | | | | | | |
| | | | | | | | | | | |
| | | | | | | | | | | |
| | | | | | | | | | | |
| | | | | | | | | | | |

Notes:

# Activity

date(s): _____

| | Initials | Time | Bible and Life | Language Arts | Math | World Studies | Science | Arts and Handicraft | Physical Activity | Outings/Life Skiill |
|---|---|---|---|---|---|---|---|---|---|---|
| _____ | | | | | | | | | | |
| _____ | | | | | | | | | | |
| _____ | | | | | | | | | | |
| _____ | | | | | | | | | | |
| _____ | | | | | | | | | | |
| _____ | | | | | | | | | | |
| _____ | | | | | | | | | | |
| _____ | | | | | | | | | | |
| _____ | | | | | | | | | | |
| _____ | | | | | | | | | | |
| _____ | | | | | | | | | | |
| _____ | | | | | | | | | | |
| _____ | | | | | | | | | | |

Notes:

# Activity

date(s): _____

| | Initials | Time | Bible and Life | Language Arts | Math | World Studies | Science | Arts and Handicraft | Physical Activity | Outings/Life Skill |
|---|---|---|---|---|---|---|---|---|---|---|
| | | | | | | | | | | |
| | | | | | | | | | | |
| | | | | | | | | | | |
| | | | | | | | | | | |
| | | | | | | | | | | |
| | | | | | | | | | | |
| | | | | | | | | | | |
| | | | | | | | | | | |
| | | | | | | | | | | |
| | | | | | | | | | | |
| | | | | | | | | | | |
| | | | | | | | | | | |
| | | | | | | | | | | |

Notes:

# Activity

date(s): _____

| | Initials | Time | Bible and Life | Language Arts | Math | World Studies | Science | Arts and Handicraft | Physical Activity | Outings/Life Skiill |
|---|---|---|---|---|---|---|---|---|---|---|
| | | | | | | | | | | |
| | | | | | | | | | | |
| | | | | | | | | | | |
| | | | | | | | | | | |
| | | | | | | | | | | |
| | | | | | | | | | | |
| | | | | | | | | | | |
| | | | | | | | | | | |
| | | | | | | | | | | |
| | | | | | | | | | | |
| | | | | | | | | | | |
| | | | | | | | | | | |
| | | | | | | | | | | |

Notes:

## Activity

date(s): _____

| | Initials | Time | Bible and Life | Language Arts | Math | World Studies | Science | Arts and Handicraft | Physical Activity | Outings/Life Skiill |
|---|---|---|---|---|---|---|---|---|---|---|
| | | | | | | | | | | |
| | | | | | | | | | | |
| | | | | | | | | | | |
| | | | | | | | | | | |
| | | | | | | | | | | |
| | | | | | | | | | | |
| | | | | | | | | | | |
| | | | | | | | | | | |
| | | | | | | | | | | |
| | | | | | | | | | | |
| | | | | | | | | | | |
| | | | | | | | | | | |
| | | | | | | | | | | |

Notes:

# Activity

date(s): _____

| | Initials | Time | Bible and Life | Language Arts | Math | World Studies | Science | Arts and Handicraft | Physical Activity | Outings/Life Skill |
|---|---|---|---|---|---|---|---|---|---|---|
| | | | | | | | | | | |
| | | | | | | | | | | |
| | | | | | | | | | | |
| | | | | | | | | | | |
| | | | | | | | | | | |
| | | | | | | | | | | |
| | | | | | | | | | | |
| | | | | | | | | | | |
| | | | | | | | | | | |
| | | | | | | | | | | |
| | | | | | | | | | | |
| | | | | | | | | | | |
| | | | | | | | | | | |

Notes:

# Activity

date(s): _____

| | Initials | Time | Bible and Life | Language Arts | Math | World Studies | Science | Arts and Handicraft | Physical Activity | Outings/Life Skiill |
|---|---|---|---|---|---|---|---|---|---|---|
| | | | | | | | | | | |
| | | | | | | | | | | |
| | | | | | | | | | | |
| | | | | | | | | | | |
| | | | | | | | | | | |
| | | | | | | | | | | |
| | | | | | | | | | | |
| | | | | | | | | | | |
| | | | | | | | | | | |
| | | | | | | | | | | |
| | | | | | | | | | | |
| | | | | | | | | | | |
| | | | | | | | | | | |

Notes:

# Activity

date(s): _____

|  | Initials | Time | Bible and Life | Language Arts | Math | World Studies | Science | Arts and Handicraft | Physical Activity | Outings/Life Skill |
|---|---|---|---|---|---|---|---|---|---|---|
| | | | | | | | | | | |
| | | | | | | | | | | |
| | | | | | | | | | | |
| | | | | | | | | | | |
| | | | | | | | | | | |
| | | | | | | | | | | |
| | | | | | | | | | | |
| | | | | | | | | | | |
| | | | | | | | | | | |
| | | | | | | | | | | |
| | | | | | | | | | | |
| | | | | | | | | | | |
| | | | | | | | | | | |

Notes:

# Activity

date(s): _____

| | Initials | Time | Bible and Life | Language Arts | Math | World Studies | Science | Arts and Handicraft | Physical Activity | Outings/Life Skill |
|---|---|---|---|---|---|---|---|---|---|---|
| | | | | | | | | | | |
| | | | | | | | | | | |
| | | | | | | | | | | |
| | | | | | | | | | | |
| | | | | | | | | | | |
| | | | | | | | | | | |
| | | | | | | | | | | |
| | | | | | | | | | | |
| | | | | | | | | | | |
| | | | | | | | | | | |
| | | | | | | | | | | |
| | | | | | | | | | | |

Notes:

# Activity

date(s): _____

| | Initials | Time | Bible and Life | Language Arts | Math | World Studies | Science | Arts and Handicraft | Physical Activity | Outings/Life Skill |
|---|---|---|---|---|---|---|---|---|---|---|
| | | | | | | | | | | |
| | | | | | | | | | | |
| | | | | | | | | | | |
| | | | | | | | | | | |
| | | | | | | | | | | |
| | | | | | | | | | | |
| | | | | | | | | | | |
| | | | | | | | | | | |
| | | | | | | | | | | |
| | | | | | | | | | | |
| | | | | | | | | | | |
| | | | | | | | | | | |
| | | | | | | | | | | |

Notes:

# Activity

date(s): _____

| | Initials | Time | Bible and Life | Language Arts | Math | World Studies | Science | Arts and Handicraft | Physical Activity | Outings/Life Skiill |
|---|---|---|---|---|---|---|---|---|---|---|
| | | | | | | | | | | |
| | | | | | | | | | | |
| | | | | | | | | | | |
| | | | | | | | | | | |
| | | | | | | | | | | |
| | | | | | | | | | | |
| | | | | | | | | | | |
| | | | | | | | | | | |
| | | | | | | | | | | |
| | | | | | | | | | | |
| | | | | | | | | | | |
| | | | | | | | | | | |
| | | | | | | | | | | |

Notes:

# Activity

date(s): _____

| | Initials | Time | Bible and Life | Language Arts | Math | World Studies | Science | Arts and Handicraft | Physical Activity | Outings/Life Skiill |
|---|---|---|---|---|---|---|---|---|---|---|
| | | | | | | | | | | |
| | | | | | | | | | | |
| | | | | | | | | | | |
| | | | | | | | | | | |
| | | | | | | | | | | |
| | | | | | | | | | | |
| | | | | | | | | | | |
| | | | | | | | | | | |
| | | | | | | | | | | |
| | | | | | | | | | | |
| | | | | | | | | | | |
| | | | | | | | | | | |
| | | | | | | | | | | |

Notes:

## Activity

date(s): _____

|  | Initials | Time | Bible and Life | Language Arts | Math | World Studies | Science | Arts and Handicraft | Physical Activity | Outings/Life Skill |
|---|---|---|---|---|---|---|---|---|---|---|
| | | | | | | | | | | |
| | | | | | | | | | | |
| | | | | | | | | | | |
| | | | | | | | | | | |
| | | | | | | | | | | |
| | | | | | | | | | | |
| | | | | | | | | | | |
| | | | | | | | | | | |
| | | | | | | | | | | |
| | | | | | | | | | | |
| | | | | | | | | | | |
| | | | | | | | | | | |
| | | | | | | | | | | |

Notes:

THE RECORD BOOK • MOMDELIGHTS.COM

# Activity

date(s): _____

| | Initials | Time | Bible and Life | Language Arts | Math | World Studies | Science | Arts and Handicraft | Physical Activity | Outings/Life Skill |
|---|---|---|---|---|---|---|---|---|---|---|
| | | | | | | | | | | |
| | | | | | | | | | | |
| | | | | | | | | | | |
| | | | | | | | | | | |
| | | | | | | | | | | |
| | | | | | | | | | | |
| | | | | | | | | | | |
| | | | | | | | | | | |
| | | | | | | | | | | |
| | | | | | | | | | | |
| | | | | | | | | | | |
| | | | | | | | | | | |
| | | | | | | | | | | |

Notes:

# Activity

date(s): _____

| | Initials | Time | Bible and Life | Language Arts | Math | World Studies | Science | Arts and Handicraft | Physical Activity | Outings/Life Skill |
|---|---|---|---|---|---|---|---|---|---|---|
| | | | | | | | | | | |
| | | | | | | | | | | |
| | | | | | | | | | | |
| | | | | | | | | | | |
| | | | | | | | | | | |
| | | | | | | | | | | |
| | | | | | | | | | | |
| | | | | | | | | | | |
| | | | | | | | | | | |
| | | | | | | | | | | |
| | | | | | | | | | | |
| | | | | | | | | | | |
| | | | | | | | | | | |

Notes:

# Activity

date(s): _____

| | Initials | Time | Bible and Life | Language Arts | Math | World Studies | Science | Arts and Handicraft | Physical Activity | Outings/Life Skill |
|---|---|---|---|---|---|---|---|---|---|---|
| | | | | | | | | | | |
| | | | | | | | | | | |
| | | | | | | | | | | |
| | | | | | | | | | | |
| | | | | | | | | | | |
| | | | | | | | | | | |
| | | | | | | | | | | |
| | | | | | | | | | | |
| | | | | | | | | | | |
| | | | | | | | | | | |
| | | | | | | | | | | |
| | | | | | | | | | | |
| | | | | | | | | | | |

Notes:

# Activity

date(s): _____

| | Initials | Time | Bible and Life | Language Arts | Math | World Studies | Science | Arts and Handicraft | Physical Activity | Outings/Life Skill |
|---|---|---|---|---|---|---|---|---|---|---|
| | | | | | | | | | | |
| | | | | | | | | | | |
| | | | | | | | | | | |
| | | | | | | | | | | |
| | | | | | | | | | | |
| | | | | | | | | | | |
| | | | | | | | | | | |
| | | | | | | | | | | |
| | | | | | | | | | | |
| | | | | | | | | | | |
| | | | | | | | | | | |
| | | | | | | | | | | |
| | | | | | | | | | | |

Notes:

"And these words which I command you today shall be in your heart. You shall teach them diligently to your children, and shall talk of them when you sit in your house, when you walk by the way, when you lie down, and when you rise up. You shall bind them as a sign on your hand, and they shall be as frontlets between your eyes. You shall write them on the doorposts of your house and on your gates."
- Deuteronomy 6:6-7

"I am much afraid that the schools will prove the very gates of hell, unless they diligently labour in explaining the Holy Scriptures, and engraving them in the hearts of youth. I advise no one to place his child where the scriptures do not reign paramount. Every institution in which means are not unceasingly occupied with the Word of God must be corrupt."
- Martin Luther

"The Bible is to American education what Homer was to Athenian education. It is our classic, the core."
- Ruth Beechick, *You Can Teach Your Child Successfully*

# Activity

date(s): _____

| | Initials | Time | Bible and Life | Language Arts | Math | World Studies | Science | Arts and Handicraft | Physical Activity | Outings/Life Skiill |
|---|---|---|---|---|---|---|---|---|---|---|
| | | | | | | | | | | |
| | | | | | | | | | | |
| | | | | | | | | | | |
| | | | | | | | | | | |
| | | | | | | | | | | |
| | | | | | | | | | | |
| | | | | | | | | | | |
| | | | | | | | | | | |
| | | | | | | | | | | |
| | | | | | | | | | | |
| | | | | | | | | | | |
| | | | | | | | | | | |
| | | | | | | | | | | |

Notes:

# Activity

date(s): _____

| | Initials | Time | Bible and Life | Language Arts | Math | World Studies | Science | Arts and Handicraft | Physical Activity | Outings/Life Skiill |
|---|---|---|---|---|---|---|---|---|---|---|
| | | | | | | | | | | |
| | | | | | | | | | | |
| | | | | | | | | | | |
| | | | | | | | | | | |
| | | | | | | | | | | |
| | | | | | | | | | | |
| | | | | | | | | | | |
| | | | | | | | | | | |
| | | | | | | | | | | |
| | | | | | | | | | | |
| | | | | | | | | | | |
| | | | | | | | | | | |
| | | | | | | | | | | |

Notes:

# Activity

date(s): _____

| | Initials | Time | Bible and Life | Language Arts | Math | World Studies | Science | Arts and Handicraft | Physical Activity | Outings/Life Skill |
|---|---|---|---|---|---|---|---|---|---|---|
| | | | | | | | | | | |
| | | | | | | | | | | |
| | | | | | | | | | | |
| | | | | | | | | | | |
| | | | | | | | | | | |
| | | | | | | | | | | |
| | | | | | | | | | | |
| | | | | | | | | | | |
| | | | | | | | | | | |
| | | | | | | | | | | |
| | | | | | | | | | | |
| | | | | | | | | | | |
| | | | | | | | | | | |

Notes:

# Activity

date(s): _____

| | Initials | Time | Bible and Life | Language Arts | Math | World Studies | Science | Arts and Handicraft | Physical Activity | Outings/Life Skill |
|---|---|---|---|---|---|---|---|---|---|---|
| | | | | | | | | | | |
| | | | | | | | | | | |
| | | | | | | | | | | |
| | | | | | | | | | | |
| | | | | | | | | | | |
| | | | | | | | | | | |
| | | | | | | | | | | |
| | | | | | | | | | | |
| | | | | | | | | | | |
| | | | | | | | | | | |
| | | | | | | | | | | |
| | | | | | | | | | | |
| | | | | | | | | | | |

Notes:

# Activity

date(s): _____

| | Initials | Time | Bible and Life | Language Arts | Math | World Studies | Science | Arts and Handicraft | Physical Activity | Outings/Life Skill |
|---|---|---|---|---|---|---|---|---|---|---|
| | | | | | | | | | | |
| | | | | | | | | | | |
| | | | | | | | | | | |
| | | | | | | | | | | |
| | | | | | | | | | | |
| | | | | | | | | | | |
| | | | | | | | | | | |
| | | | | | | | | | | |
| | | | | | | | | | | |
| | | | | | | | | | | |
| | | | | | | | | | | |
| | | | | | | | | | | |
| | | | | | | | | | | |

Notes:

# Activity

date(s): _____

|  | Initials | Time | Bible and Life | Language Arts | Math | World Studies | Science | Arts and Handicraft | Physical Activity | Outings/Life Skill |
|---|---|---|---|---|---|---|---|---|---|---|
| | | | | | | | | | | |
| | | | | | | | | | | |
| | | | | | | | | | | |
| | | | | | | | | | | |
| | | | | | | | | | | |
| | | | | | | | | | | |
| | | | | | | | | | | |
| | | | | | | | | | | |
| | | | | | | | | | | |
| | | | | | | | | | | |
| | | | | | | | | | | |
| | | | | | | | | | | |
| | | | | | | | | | | |

Notes:

# Activity

date(s): _____

| | Initials | Time | Bible and Life | Language Arts | Math | World Studies | Science | Arts and Handicraft | Physical Activity | Outings/Life Skiill |
|---|---|---|---|---|---|---|---|---|---|---|

Notes:

# Activity

date(s): _____

| | Initials | Time | Bible and Life | Language Arts | Math | World Studies | Science | Arts and Handicraft | Physical Activity | Outings/Life Skill |
|---|---|---|---|---|---|---|---|---|---|---|
| _____ | | | | | | | | | | |
| _____ | | | | | | | | | | |
| _____ | | | | | | | | | | |
| _____ | | | | | | | | | | |
| _____ | | | | | | | | | | |
| _____ | | | | | | | | | | |
| _____ | | | | | | | | | | |
| _____ | | | | | | | | | | |
| _____ | | | | | | | | | | |
| _____ | | | | | | | | | | |
| _____ | | | | | | | | | | |
| _____ | | | | | | | | | | |
| _____ | | | | | | | | | | |

Notes:

## Activity

date(s): _____

| | Initials | Time | Bible and Life | Language Arts | Math | World Studies | Science | Arts and Handicraft | Physical Activity | Outings/Life Skill |
|---|---|---|---|---|---|---|---|---|---|---|
| | | | | | | | | | | |
| | | | | | | | | | | |
| | | | | | | | | | | |
| | | | | | | | | | | |
| | | | | | | | | | | |
| | | | | | | | | | | |
| | | | | | | | | | | |
| | | | | | | | | | | |
| | | | | | | | | | | |
| | | | | | | | | | | |
| | | | | | | | | | | |
| | | | | | | | | | | |
| | | | | | | | | | | |

Notes:

# Activity

date(s): _____

|  | Initials | Time | Bible and Life | Language Arts | Math | World Studies | Science | Arts and Handicraft | Physical Activity | Outings/Life Skiill |
|---|---|---|---|---|---|---|---|---|---|---|
|  |  |  |  |  |  |  |  |  |  |  |
|  |  |  |  |  |  |  |  |  |  |  |
|  |  |  |  |  |  |  |  |  |  |  |
|  |  |  |  |  |  |  |  |  |  |  |
|  |  |  |  |  |  |  |  |  |  |  |
|  |  |  |  |  |  |  |  |  |  |  |
|  |  |  |  |  |  |  |  |  |  |  |
|  |  |  |  |  |  |  |  |  |  |  |
|  |  |  |  |  |  |  |  |  |  |  |
|  |  |  |  |  |  |  |  |  |  |  |
|  |  |  |  |  |  |  |  |  |  |  |
|  |  |  |  |  |  |  |  |  |  |  |
|  |  |  |  |  |  |  |  |  |  |  |

Notes:

## Activity

date(s): _____

| | Initials | Time | Bible and Life | Language Arts | Math | World Studies | Science | Arts and Handicraft | Physical Activity | Outings/Life Skill |
|---|---|---|---|---|---|---|---|---|---|---|
| | | | | | | | | | | |
| | | | | | | | | | | |
| | | | | | | | | | | |
| | | | | | | | | | | |
| | | | | | | | | | | |
| | | | | | | | | | | |
| | | | | | | | | | | |
| | | | | | | | | | | |
| | | | | | | | | | | |
| | | | | | | | | | | |
| | | | | | | | | | | |
| | | | | | | | | | | |
| | | | | | | | | | | |

Notes:

## Activity        date(s): _____

|  | Initials | Time | Bible and Life | Language Arts | Math | World Studies | Science | Arts and Handicraft | Physical Activity | Outings/Life Skiill |
|---|---|---|---|---|---|---|---|---|---|---|
|  |  |  |  |  |  |  |  |  |  |  |
|  |  |  |  |  |  |  |  |  |  |  |
|  |  |  |  |  |  |  |  |  |  |  |
|  |  |  |  |  |  |  |  |  |  |  |
|  |  |  |  |  |  |  |  |  |  |  |
|  |  |  |  |  |  |  |  |  |  |  |
|  |  |  |  |  |  |  |  |  |  |  |
|  |  |  |  |  |  |  |  |  |  |  |
|  |  |  |  |  |  |  |  |  |  |  |
|  |  |  |  |  |  |  |  |  |  |  |
|  |  |  |  |  |  |  |  |  |  |  |
|  |  |  |  |  |  |  |  |  |  |  |
|  |  |  |  |  |  |  |  |  |  |  |

Notes:

# Activity

date(s): _____

| | Initials | Time | Bible and Life | Language Arts | Math | World Studies | Science | Arts and Handicraft | Physical Activity | Outings/Life Skill |
|---|---|---|---|---|---|---|---|---|---|---|
| | | | | | | | | | | |
| | | | | | | | | | | |
| | | | | | | | | | | |
| | | | | | | | | | | |
| | | | | | | | | | | |
| | | | | | | | | | | |
| | | | | | | | | | | |
| | | | | | | | | | | |
| | | | | | | | | | | |
| | | | | | | | | | | |
| | | | | | | | | | | |
| | | | | | | | | | | |
| | | | | | | | | | | |

Notes:

# Activity

date(s): _____

| | Initials | Time | Bible and Life | Language Arts | Math | World Studies | Science | Arts and Handicraft | Physical Activity | Outings/Life Skill |
|---|---|---|---|---|---|---|---|---|---|---|
| | | | | | | | | | | |
| | | | | | | | | | | |
| | | | | | | | | | | |
| | | | | | | | | | | |
| | | | | | | | | | | |
| | | | | | | | | | | |
| | | | | | | | | | | |
| | | | | | | | | | | |
| | | | | | | | | | | |
| | | | | | | | | | | |
| | | | | | | | | | | |
| | | | | | | | | | | |
| | | | | | | | | | | |

Notes:

# Activity

date(s): _____

|  | Initials | Time | Bible and Life | Language Arts | Math | World Studies | Science | Arts and Handicraft | Physical Activity | Outings/Life Skill |
|---|---|---|---|---|---|---|---|---|---|---|

Notes:

# Activity

date(s): _____

| | Initials | Time | Bible and Life | Language Arts | Math | World Studies | Science | Arts and Handicraft | Physical Activity | Outings/Life Skiill |
|---|---|---|---|---|---|---|---|---|---|---|
| | | | | | | | | | | |
| | | | | | | | | | | |
| | | | | | | | | | | |
| | | | | | | | | | | |
| | | | | | | | | | | |
| | | | | | | | | | | |
| | | | | | | | | | | |
| | | | | | | | | | | |
| | | | | | | | | | | |
| | | | | | | | | | | |
| | | | | | | | | | | |
| | | | | | | | | | | |
| | | | | | | | | | | |

Notes:

# Activity

date(s): _____

| | Initials | Time | Bible and Life | Language Arts | Math | World Studies | Science | Arts and Handicraft | Physical Activity | Outings/Life Skill |
|---|---|---|---|---|---|---|---|---|---|---|
| | | | | | | | | | | |
| | | | | | | | | | | |
| | | | | | | | | | | |
| | | | | | | | | | | |
| | | | | | | | | | | |
| | | | | | | | | | | |
| | | | | | | | | | | |
| | | | | | | | | | | |
| | | | | | | | | | | |
| | | | | | | | | | | |
| | | | | | | | | | | |
| | | | | | | | | | | |
| | | | | | | | | | | |

Notes:

# Activity

date(s): _____

| | Initials | Time | Bible and Life | Language Arts | Math | World Studies | Science | Arts and Handicraft | Physical Activity | Outings/Life Skill |
|---|---|---|---|---|---|---|---|---|---|---|
| | | | | | | | | | | |
| | | | | | | | | | | |
| | | | | | | | | | | |
| | | | | | | | | | | |
| | | | | | | | | | | |
| | | | | | | | | | | |
| | | | | | | | | | | |
| | | | | | | | | | | |
| | | | | | | | | | | |
| | | | | | | | | | | |
| | | | | | | | | | | |
| | | | | | | | | | | |
| | | | | | | | | | | |

Notes:

# Activity

date(s): _____

| | Initials | Time | Bible and Life | Language Arts | Math | World Studies | Science | Arts and Handicraft | Physical Activity | Outings/Life Skill |
|---|---|---|---|---|---|---|---|---|---|---|
| | | | | | | | | | | |
| | | | | | | | | | | |
| | | | | | | | | | | |
| | | | | | | | | | | |
| | | | | | | | | | | |
| | | | | | | | | | | |
| | | | | | | | | | | |
| | | | | | | | | | | |
| | | | | | | | | | | |
| | | | | | | | | | | |
| | | | | | | | | | | |
| | | | | | | | | | | |
| | | | | | | | | | | |

Notes:

# Activity

date(s): _____

| | Initials | Time | Bible and Life | Language Arts | Math | World Studies | Science | Arts and Handicraft | Physical Activity | Outings/Life Skill |
|---|---|---|---|---|---|---|---|---|---|---|
| _____ | | | | | | | | | | |
| _____ | | | | | | | | | | |
| _____ | | | | | | | | | | |
| _____ | | | | | | | | | | |
| _____ | | | | | | | | | | |
| _____ | | | | | | | | | | |
| _____ | | | | | | | | | | |
| _____ | | | | | | | | | | |
| _____ | | | | | | | | | | |
| _____ | | | | | | | | | | |
| _____ | | | | | | | | | | |
| _____ | | | | | | | | | | |
| _____ | | | | | | | | | | |

Notes:

# Activity

date(s): _____

| | Initials | Time | Bible and Life | Language Arts | Math | World Studies | Science | Arts and Handicraft | Physical Activity | Outings/Life Skill |
|---|---|---|---|---|---|---|---|---|---|---|
| | | | | | | | | | | |
| | | | | | | | | | | |
| | | | | | | | | | | |
| | | | | | | | | | | |
| | | | | | | | | | | |
| | | | | | | | | | | |
| | | | | | | | | | | |
| | | | | | | | | | | |
| | | | | | | | | | | |
| | | | | | | | | | | |
| | | | | | | | | | | |
| | | | | | | | | | | |
| | | | | | | | | | | |

Notes:

# Activity

date(s): _____

| | Initials | Time | Bible and Life | Language Arts | Math | World Studies | Science | Arts and Handicraft | Physical Activity | Outings/Life Skill |
|---|---|---|---|---|---|---|---|---|---|---|
| _____ | | | | | | | | | | |
| _____ | | | | | | | | | | |
| _____ | | | | | | | | | | |
| _____ | | | | | | | | | | |
| _____ | | | | | | | | | | |
| _____ | | | | | | | | | | |
| _____ | | | | | | | | | | |
| _____ | | | | | | | | | | |
| _____ | | | | | | | | | | |
| _____ | | | | | | | | | | |
| _____ | | | | | | | | | | |
| _____ | | | | | | | | | | |
| _____ | | | | | | | | | | |

Notes:

# Activity

date(s): _____

|  | Initials | Time | Bible and Life | Language Arts | Math | World Studies | Science | Arts and Handicraft | Physical Activity | Outings/Life Skiill |
|---|---|---|---|---|---|---|---|---|---|---|
| | | | | | | | | | | |
| | | | | | | | | | | |
| | | | | | | | | | | |
| | | | | | | | | | | |
| | | | | | | | | | | |
| | | | | | | | | | | |
| | | | | | | | | | | |
| | | | | | | | | | | |
| | | | | | | | | | | |
| | | | | | | | | | | |
| | | | | | | | | | | |
| | | | | | | | | | | |
| | | | | | | | | | | |

Notes:

# Activity

date(s): _____

| | Initials | Time | Bible and Life | Language Arts | Math | World Studies | Science | Arts and Handicraft | Physical Activity | Outings/Life Skill |
|---|---|---|---|---|---|---|---|---|---|---|
| | | | | | | | | | | |
| | | | | | | | | | | |
| | | | | | | | | | | |
| | | | | | | | | | | |
| | | | | | | | | | | |
| | | | | | | | | | | |
| | | | | | | | | | | |
| | | | | | | | | | | |
| | | | | | | | | | | |
| | | | | | | | | | | |
| | | | | | | | | | | |
| | | | | | | | | | | |
| | | | | | | | | | | |

Notes:

# Activity

date(s): _____

| | Initials | Time | Bible and Life | Language Arts | Math | World Studies | Science | Arts and Handicraft | Physical Activity | Outings/Life Skill |
|---|---|---|---|---|---|---|---|---|---|---|
| | | | | | | | | | | |
| | | | | | | | | | | |
| | | | | | | | | | | |
| | | | | | | | | | | |
| | | | | | | | | | | |
| | | | | | | | | | | |
| | | | | | | | | | | |
| | | | | | | | | | | |
| | | | | | | | | | | |
| | | | | | | | | | | |
| | | | | | | | | | | |
| | | | | | | | | | | |

Notes:

# Activity

date(s): _____

| | Initials | Time | Bible and Life | Language Arts | Math | World Studies | Science | Arts and Handicraft | Physical Activity | Outings/Life Skiill |
|---|---|---|---|---|---|---|---|---|---|---|
| | | | | | | | | | | |
| | | | | | | | | | | |
| | | | | | | | | | | |
| | | | | | | | | | | |
| | | | | | | | | | | |
| | | | | | | | | | | |
| | | | | | | | | | | |
| | | | | | | | | | | |
| | | | | | | | | | | |
| | | | | | | | | | | |
| | | | | | | | | | | |
| | | | | | | | | | | |
| | | | | | | | | | | |

Notes:

# Activity

date(s): _____

| | Initials | Time | Bible and Life | Language Arts | Math | World Studies | Science | Arts and Handicraft | Physical Activity | Outings/Life Skill |
|---|---|---|---|---|---|---|---|---|---|---|
| | | | | | | | | | | |
| | | | | | | | | | | |
| | | | | | | | | | | |
| | | | | | | | | | | |
| | | | | | | | | | | |
| | | | | | | | | | | |
| | | | | | | | | | | |
| | | | | | | | | | | |
| | | | | | | | | | | |
| | | | | | | | | | | |
| | | | | | | | | | | |
| | | | | | | | | | | |
| | | | | | | | | | | |

Notes:

## Activity

date(s): _____

| | Initials | Time | Bible and Life | Language Arts | Math | World Studies | Science | Arts and Handicraft | Physical Activity | Outings/Life Skill |
|---|---|---|---|---|---|---|---|---|---|---|
| | | | | | | | | | | |
| | | | | | | | | | | |
| | | | | | | | | | | |
| | | | | | | | | | | |
| | | | | | | | | | | |
| | | | | | | | | | | |
| | | | | | | | | | | |
| | | | | | | | | | | |
| | | | | | | | | | | |
| | | | | | | | | | | |
| | | | | | | | | | | |
| | | | | | | | | | | |
| | | | | | | | | | | |
| | | | | | | | | | | |

Notes:

# Activity

date(s): _____

| | Initials | Time | Bible and Life | Language Arts | Math | World Studies | Science | Arts and Handicraft | Physical Activity | Outings/Life Skill |
|---|---|---|---|---|---|---|---|---|---|---|
| | | | | | | | | | | |
| | | | | | | | | | | |
| | | | | | | | | | | |
| | | | | | | | | | | |
| | | | | | | | | | | |
| | | | | | | | | | | |
| | | | | | | | | | | |
| | | | | | | | | | | |
| | | | | | | | | | | |
| | | | | | | | | | | |
| | | | | | | | | | | |
| | | | | | | | | | | |
| | | | | | | | | | | |

Notes:

# Activity

date(s): _____

| | Initials | Time | Bible and Life | Language Arts | Math | World Studies | Science | Arts and Handicraft | Physical Activity | Outings/Life Skill |
|---|---|---|---|---|---|---|---|---|---|---|
| _____ | | | | | | | | | | |
| _____ | | | | | | | | | | |
| _____ | | | | | | | | | | |
| _____ | | | | | | | | | | |
| _____ | | | | | | | | | | |
| _____ | | | | | | | | | | |
| _____ | | | | | | | | | | |
| _____ | | | | | | | | | | |
| _____ | | | | | | | | | | |
| _____ | | | | | | | | | | |
| _____ | | | | | | | | | | |
| _____ | | | | | | | | | | |
| _____ | | | | | | | | | | |

Notes:

# Activity

date(s): _____

|  | Initials | Time | Bible and Life | Language Arts | Math | World Studies | Science | Arts and Handicraft | Physical Activity | Outings/Life Skill |
|---|---|---|---|---|---|---|---|---|---|---|
| | | | | | | | | | | |
| | | | | | | | | | | |
| | | | | | | | | | | |
| | | | | | | | | | | |
| | | | | | | | | | | |
| | | | | | | | | | | |
| | | | | | | | | | | |
| | | | | | | | | | | |
| | | | | | | | | | | |
| | | | | | | | | | | |
| | | | | | | | | | | |
| | | | | | | | | | | |

Notes:

# Activity

date(s): _____

|  | Initials | Time | Bible and Life | Language Arts | Math | World Studies | Science | Arts and Handicraft | Physical Activity | Outings/Life Skiill |
|---|---|---|---|---|---|---|---|---|---|---|
| ................................................................ | | | | | | | | | | |
| ................................................................ | | | | | | | | | | |
| ................................................................ | | | | | | | | | | |
| ................................................................ | | | | | | | | | | |
| ................................................................ | | | | | | | | | | |
| ................................................................ | | | | | | | | | | |
| ................................................................ | | | | | | | | | | |
| ................................................................ | | | | | | | | | | |
| ................................................................ | | | | | | | | | | |
| ................................................................ | | | | | | | | | | |
| ................................................................ | | | | | | | | | | |
| ................................................................ | | | | | | | | | | |
| ................................................................ | | | | | | | | | | |

Notes:

# Activity

date(s): _____

| | Initials | Time | Bible and Life | Language Arts | Math | World Studies | Science | Arts and Handicraft | Physical Activity | Outings/Life Skill |
|---|---|---|---|---|---|---|---|---|---|---|
| | | | | | | | | | | |
| | | | | | | | | | | |
| | | | | | | | | | | |
| | | | | | | | | | | |
| | | | | | | | | | | |
| | | | | | | | | | | |
| | | | | | | | | | | |
| | | | | | | | | | | |
| | | | | | | | | | | |
| | | | | | | | | | | |
| | | | | | | | | | | |
| | | | | | | | | | | |
| | | | | | | | | | | |

Notes:

# Activity

date(s): _____

| | Initials | Time | Bible and Life | Language Arts | Math | World Studies | Science | Arts and Handicraft | Physical Activity | Outings/Life Skiill |
|---|---|---|---|---|---|---|---|---|---|---|

**Notes:**

# Activity

date(s): _____

| | Initials | Time | Bible and Life | Language Arts | Math | World Studies | Science | Arts and Handicraft | Physical Activity | Outings/Life Skill |
|---|---|---|---|---|---|---|---|---|---|---|
| | | | | | | | | | | |
| | | | | | | | | | | |
| | | | | | | | | | | |
| | | | | | | | | | | |
| | | | | | | | | | | |
| | | | | | | | | | | |
| | | | | | | | | | | |
| | | | | | | | | | | |
| | | | | | | | | | | |
| | | | | | | | | | | |
| | | | | | | | | | | |
| | | | | | | | | | | |
| | | | | | | | | | | |

Notes:

# Activity

date(s): _____

| | Initials | Time | Bible and Life | Language Arts | Math | World Studies | Science | Arts and Handicraft | Physical Activity | Outings/Life Skill |
|---|---|---|---|---|---|---|---|---|---|---|
| | | | | | | | | | | |
| | | | | | | | | | | |
| | | | | | | | | | | |
| | | | | | | | | | | |
| | | | | | | | | | | |
| | | | | | | | | | | |
| | | | | | | | | | | |
| | | | | | | | | | | |
| | | | | | | | | | | |
| | | | | | | | | | | |
| | | | | | | | | | | |
| | | | | | | | | | | |
| | | | | | | | | | | |

Notes:

# Activity

date(s): _____

|  | Initials | Time | Bible and Life | Language Arts | Math | World Studies | Science | Arts and Handicraft | Physical Activity | Outings/Life Skiill |
|---|---|---|---|---|---|---|---|---|---|---|
| | | | | | | | | | | |
| | | | | | | | | | | |
| | | | | | | | | | | |
| | | | | | | | | | | |
| | | | | | | | | | | |
| | | | | | | | | | | |
| | | | | | | | | | | |
| | | | | | | | | | | |
| | | | | | | | | | | |
| | | | | | | | | | | |
| | | | | | | | | | | |
| | | | | | | | | | | |

Notes:

"But ye, beloved, building up yourselves on your most holy faith, praying in the Holy Ghost, Keep yourselves in the love of God, looking for the mercy of our Lord Jesus Christ unto eternal life. And of some have compassion, making a difference"
- Jude 1:20-22

"The parent's chief care is, that that which they supply shall be wholesome and nourishing whether in the way of picture books, lessons, playmates, bread and milk, or mother's love."
- Charlotte Mason

"An alarming number of parents appear to have little confidence in their ability to "teach" their children. We should help parents understand the overriding importance of incidental teaching in the context of warm, consistent companionship. Such caring is usually the greatest teaching, especially if caring means sharing in the activities of the home."
— Raymond S. Moore, *School Can Wait*

# Activity

date(s): _____

| | Initials | Time | Bible and Life | Language Arts | Math | World Studies | Science | Arts and Handicraft | Physical Activity | Outings/Life Skiill |
|---|---|---|---|---|---|---|---|---|---|---|

Notes:

# Activity

date(s): _____

|  | Initials | Time | Bible and Life | Language Arts | Math | World Studies | Science | Arts and Handicraft | Physical Activity | Outings/Life Skill |
|---|---|---|---|---|---|---|---|---|---|---|
| ................................................. | | | | | | | | | | |
| ................................................. | | | | | | | | | | |
| ................................................. | | | | | | | | | | |
| ................................................. | | | | | | | | | | |
| ................................................. | | | | | | | | | | |
| ................................................. | | | | | | | | | | |
| ................................................. | | | | | | | | | | |
| ................................................. | | | | | | | | | | |
| ................................................. | | | | | | | | | | |
| ................................................. | | | | | | | | | | |
| ................................................. | | | | | | | | | | |
| ................................................. | | | | | | | | | | |
| ................................................. | | | | | | | | | | |

Notes:

# Activity

date(s): _____

| | Initials | Time | Bible and Life | Language Arts | Math | World Studies | Science | Arts and Handicraft | Physical Activity | Outings/Life Skill |
|---|---|---|---|---|---|---|---|---|---|---|
| | | | | | | | | | | |
| | | | | | | | | | | |
| | | | | | | | | | | |
| | | | | | | | | | | |
| | | | | | | | | | | |
| | | | | | | | | | | |
| | | | | | | | | | | |
| | | | | | | | | | | |
| | | | | | | | | | | |
| | | | | | | | | | | |
| | | | | | | | | | | |
| | | | | | | | | | | |

Notes:

# Activity

date(s): _____

| | Initials | Time | Bible and Life | Language Arts | Math | World Studies | Science | Arts and Handicraft | Physical Activity | Outings/Life Skill |
|---|---|---|---|---|---|---|---|---|---|---|
| | | | | | | | | | | |
| | | | | | | | | | | |
| | | | | | | | | | | |
| | | | | | | | | | | |
| | | | | | | | | | | |
| | | | | | | | | | | |
| | | | | | | | | | | |
| | | | | | | | | | | |
| | | | | | | | | | | |
| | | | | | | | | | | |
| | | | | | | | | | | |
| | | | | | | | | | | |
| | | | | | | | | | | |

Notes:

# Activity

date(s): _____

|  | Initials | Time | Bible and Life | Language Arts | Math | World Studies | Science | Arts and Handicraft | Physical Activity | Outings/Life Skill |
|---|---|---|---|---|---|---|---|---|---|---|
| | | | | | | | | | | |
| | | | | | | | | | | |
| | | | | | | | | | | |
| | | | | | | | | | | |
| | | | | | | | | | | |
| | | | | | | | | | | |
| | | | | | | | | | | |
| | | | | | | | | | | |
| | | | | | | | | | | |
| | | | | | | | | | | |
| | | | | | | | | | | |
| | | | | | | | | | | |
| | | | | | | | | | | |

Notes:

# Activity

date(s): _____

| | Initials | Time | Bible and Life | Language Arts | Math | World Studies | Science | Arts and Handicraft | Physical Activity | Outings/Life Skill |
|---|---|---|---|---|---|---|---|---|---|---|
| | | | | | | | | | | |
| | | | | | | | | | | |
| | | | | | | | | | | |
| | | | | | | | | | | |
| | | | | | | | | | | |
| | | | | | | | | | | |
| | | | | | | | | | | |
| | | | | | | | | | | |
| | | | | | | | | | | |
| | | | | | | | | | | |
| | | | | | | | | | | |
| | | | | | | | | | | |
| | | | | | | | | | | |
| | | | | | | | | | | |

Notes:

# Activity

date(s): _____

| | Initials | Time | Bible and Life | Language Arts | Math | World Studies | Science | Arts and Handicraft | Physical Activity | Outings/Life Skill |
|---|---|---|---|---|---|---|---|---|---|---|
| | | | | | | | | | | |
| | | | | | | | | | | |
| | | | | | | | | | | |
| | | | | | | | | | | |
| | | | | | | | | | | |
| | | | | | | | | | | |
| | | | | | | | | | | |
| | | | | | | | | | | |
| | | | | | | | | | | |
| | | | | | | | | | | |
| | | | | | | | | | | |
| | | | | | | | | | | |
| | | | | | | | | | | |

Notes:

# Activity

date(s): _____

|  | Initials | Time | Bible and Life | Language Arts | Math | World Studies | Science | Arts and Handicraft | Physical Activity | Outings/Life Skill |
|---|---|---|---|---|---|---|---|---|---|---|
| | | | | | | | | | | |
| | | | | | | | | | | |
| | | | | | | | | | | |
| | | | | | | | | | | |
| | | | | | | | | | | |
| | | | | | | | | | | |
| | | | | | | | | | | |
| | | | | | | | | | | |
| | | | | | | | | | | |
| | | | | | | | | | | |
| | | | | | | | | | | |
| | | | | | | | | | | |
| | | | | | | | | | | |
| | | | | | | | | | | |

Notes:

# Activity

date(s): _____

|  | Initials | Time | Bible and Life | Language Arts | Math | World Studies | Science | Arts and Handicraft | Physical Activity | Outings/Life Skill |
|---|---|---|---|---|---|---|---|---|---|---|
| | | | | | | | | | | |
| | | | | | | | | | | |
| | | | | | | | | | | |
| | | | | | | | | | | |
| | | | | | | | | | | |
| | | | | | | | | | | |
| | | | | | | | | | | |
| | | | | | | | | | | |
| | | | | | | | | | | |
| | | | | | | | | | | |
| | | | | | | | | | | |
| | | | | | | | | | | |
| | | | | | | | | | | |

Notes:

# Activity

date(s): _____

| | Initials | Time | Bible and Life | Language Arts | Math | World Studies | Science | Arts and Handicraft | Physical Activity | Outings/Life Skill |
|---|---|---|---|---|---|---|---|---|---|---|
| | | | | | | | | | | |
| | | | | | | | | | | |
| | | | | | | | | | | |
| | | | | | | | | | | |
| | | | | | | | | | | |
| | | | | | | | | | | |
| | | | | | | | | | | |
| | | | | | | | | | | |
| | | | | | | | | | | |
| | | | | | | | | | | |
| | | | | | | | | | | |
| | | | | | | | | | | |

Notes:

# Activity

date(s): _____

| | Initials | Time | Bible and Life | Language Arts | Math | World Studies | Science | Arts and Handicraft | Physical Activity | Outings/Life Skill |
|---|---|---|---|---|---|---|---|---|---|---|
| | | | | | | | | | | |
| | | | | | | | | | | |
| | | | | | | | | | | |
| | | | | | | | | | | |
| | | | | | | | | | | |
| | | | | | | | | | | |
| | | | | | | | | | | |
| | | | | | | | | | | |
| | | | | | | | | | | |
| | | | | | | | | | | |
| | | | | | | | | | | |
| | | | | | | | | | | |
| | | | | | | | | | | |

Notes:

# Activity

date(s): _____

| | Initials | Time | Bible and Life | Language Arts | Math | World Studies | Science | Arts and Handicraft | Physical Activity | Outings/Life Skill |
|---|---|---|---|---|---|---|---|---|---|---|
| | | | | | | | | | | |
| | | | | | | | | | | |
| | | | | | | | | | | |
| | | | | | | | | | | |
| | | | | | | | | | | |
| | | | | | | | | | | |
| | | | | | | | | | | |
| | | | | | | | | | | |
| | | | | | | | | | | |
| | | | | | | | | | | |
| | | | | | | | | | | |
| | | | | | | | | | | |
| | | | | | | | | | | |

Notes:

# Activity

date(s): _____

| | Initials | Time | Bible and Life | Language Arts | Math | World Studies | Science | Arts and Handicraft | Physical Activity | Outings/Life Skill |
|---|---|---|---|---|---|---|---|---|---|---|
| | | | | | | | | | | |
| | | | | | | | | | | |
| | | | | | | | | | | |
| | | | | | | | | | | |
| | | | | | | | | | | |
| | | | | | | | | | | |
| | | | | | | | | | | |
| | | | | | | | | | | |
| | | | | | | | | | | |
| | | | | | | | | | | |
| | | | | | | | | | | |
| | | | | | | | | | | |

Notes:

# Activity

date(s): _____

| | Initials | Time | Bible and Life | Language Arts | Math | World Studies | Science | Arts and Handicraft | Physical Activity | Outings/Life Skill |
|---|---|---|---|---|---|---|---|---|---|---|
| | | | | | | | | | | |
| | | | | | | | | | | |
| | | | | | | | | | | |
| | | | | | | | | | | |
| | | | | | | | | | | |
| | | | | | | | | | | |
| | | | | | | | | | | |
| | | | | | | | | | | |
| | | | | | | | | | | |
| | | | | | | | | | | |
| | | | | | | | | | | |
| | | | | | | | | | | |
| | | | | | | | | | | |

Notes:

# Activity

date(s): _____

| | Initials | Time | Bible and Life | Language Arts | Math | World Studies | Science | Arts and Handicraft | Physical Activity | Outings/Life Skill |
|---|---|---|---|---|---|---|---|---|---|---|
| | | | | | | | | | | |
| | | | | | | | | | | |
| | | | | | | | | | | |
| | | | | | | | | | | |
| | | | | | | | | | | |
| | | | | | | | | | | |
| | | | | | | | | | | |
| | | | | | | | | | | |
| | | | | | | | | | | |
| | | | | | | | | | | |
| | | | | | | | | | | |
| | | | | | | | | | | |
| | | | | | | | | | | |

Notes:

# Activity

date(s): _____

| | Initials | Time | Bible and Life | Language Arts | Math | World Studies | Science | Arts and Handicraft | Physical Activity | Outings/Life Skill |
|---|---|---|---|---|---|---|---|---|---|---|
| | | | | | | | | | | |
| | | | | | | | | | | |
| | | | | | | | | | | |
| | | | | | | | | | | |
| | | | | | | | | | | |
| | | | | | | | | | | |
| | | | | | | | | | | |
| | | | | | | | | | | |
| | | | | | | | | | | |
| | | | | | | | | | | |
| | | | | | | | | | | |
| | | | | | | | | | | |
| | | | | | | | | | | |

Notes:

# Activity

date(s): _____

|  | Initials | Time | Bible and Life | Language Arts | Math | World Studies | Science | Arts and Handicraft | Physical Activity | Outings/Life Skill |
|---|---|---|---|---|---|---|---|---|---|---|
| | | | | | | | | | | |
| | | | | | | | | | | |
| | | | | | | | | | | |
| | | | | | | | | | | |
| | | | | | | | | | | |
| | | | | | | | | | | |
| | | | | | | | | | | |
| | | | | | | | | | | |
| | | | | | | | | | | |
| | | | | | | | | | | |
| | | | | | | | | | | |
| | | | | | | | | | | |
| | | | | | | | | | | |

Notes:

# Activity

date(s): _____

|  | Initials | Time | Bible and Life | Language Arts | Math | World Studies | Science | Arts and Handicraft | Physical Activity | Outings/Life Skill |
|---|---|---|---|---|---|---|---|---|---|---|
| | | | | | | | | | | |
| | | | | | | | | | | |
| | | | | | | | | | | |
| | | | | | | | | | | |
| | | | | | | | | | | |
| | | | | | | | | | | |
| | | | | | | | | | | |
| | | | | | | | | | | |
| | | | | | | | | | | |
| | | | | | | | | | | |
| | | | | | | | | | | |
| | | | | | | | | | | |
| | | | | | | | | | | |
| | | | | | | | | | | |

Notes:

# Activity

date(s): _____

| | Initials | Time | Bible and Life | Language Arts | Math | World Studies | Science | Arts and Handicraft | Physical Activity | Outings/Life Skill |
|---|---|---|---|---|---|---|---|---|---|---|
| _____ | | | | | | | | | | |
| _____ | | | | | | | | | | |
| _____ | | | | | | | | | | |
| _____ | | | | | | | | | | |
| _____ | | | | | | | | | | |
| _____ | | | | | | | | | | |
| _____ | | | | | | | | | | |
| _____ | | | | | | | | | | |
| _____ | | | | | | | | | | |
| _____ | | | | | | | | | | |
| _____ | | | | | | | | | | |
| _____ | | | | | | | | | | |
| _____ | | | | | | | | | | |

Notes:

# Activity

date(s): _____

| | Initials | Time | Bible and Life | Language Arts | Math | World Studies | Science | Arts and Handicraft | Physical Activity | Outings/Life Skill |
|---|---|---|---|---|---|---|---|---|---|---|
| | | | | | | | | | | |
| | | | | | | | | | | |
| | | | | | | | | | | |
| | | | | | | | | | | |
| | | | | | | | | | | |
| | | | | | | | | | | |
| | | | | | | | | | | |
| | | | | | | | | | | |
| | | | | | | | | | | |
| | | | | | | | | | | |
| | | | | | | | | | | |
| | | | | | | | | | | |
| | | | | | | | | | | |

Notes:

# Activity

date(s): _____

| | Initials | Time | Bible and Life | Language Arts | Math | World Studies | Science | Arts and Handicraft | Physical Activity | Outings/Life Skill |
|---|---|---|---|---|---|---|---|---|---|---|
| | | | | | | | | | | |
| | | | | | | | | | | |
| | | | | | | | | | | |
| | | | | | | | | | | |
| | | | | | | | | | | |
| | | | | | | | | | | |
| | | | | | | | | | | |
| | | | | | | | | | | |
| | | | | | | | | | | |
| | | | | | | | | | | |
| | | | | | | | | | | |
| | | | | | | | | | | |

Notes:

# Activity

date(s): _____

| | Initials | Time | Bible and Life | Language Arts | Math | World Studies | Science | Arts and Handicraft | Physical Activity | Outings/Life Skill |
|---|---|---|---|---|---|---|---|---|---|---|
| | | | | | | | | | | |
| | | | | | | | | | | |
| | | | | | | | | | | |
| | | | | | | | | | | |
| | | | | | | | | | | |
| | | | | | | | | | | |
| | | | | | | | | | | |
| | | | | | | | | | | |
| | | | | | | | | | | |
| | | | | | | | | | | |
| | | | | | | | | | | |
| | | | | | | | | | | |
| | | | | | | | | | | |

Notes:

# Activity

date(s): _____

| | Initials | Time | Bible and Life | Language Arts | Math | World Studies | Science | Arts and Handicraft | Physical Activity | Outings/Life Skill |
|---|---|---|---|---|---|---|---|---|---|---|
| | | | | | | | | | | |
| | | | | | | | | | | |
| | | | | | | | | | | |
| | | | | | | | | | | |
| | | | | | | | | | | |
| | | | | | | | | | | |
| | | | | | | | | | | |
| | | | | | | | | | | |
| | | | | | | | | | | |
| | | | | | | | | | | |
| | | | | | | | | | | |
| | | | | | | | | | | |
| | | | | | | | | | | |

Notes:

# Activity

date(s): _____

| | Initials | Time | Bible and Life | Language Arts | Math | World Studies | Science | Arts and Handicraft | Physical Activity | Outings/Life Skill |
|---|---|---|---|---|---|---|---|---|---|---|
| | | | | | | | | | | |
| | | | | | | | | | | |
| | | | | | | | | | | |
| | | | | | | | | | | |
| | | | | | | | | | | |
| | | | | | | | | | | |
| | | | | | | | | | | |
| | | | | | | | | | | |
| | | | | | | | | | | |
| | | | | | | | | | | |
| | | | | | | | | | | |
| | | | | | | | | | | |
| | | | | | | | | | | |

Notes:

# Activity

date(s): _____

|  | Initials | Time | Bible and Life | Language Arts | Math | World Studies | Science | Arts and Handicraft | Physical Activity | Outings/Life Skill |
|---|---|---|---|---|---|---|---|---|---|---|
| | | | | | | | | | | |
| | | | | | | | | | | |
| | | | | | | | | | | |
| | | | | | | | | | | |
| | | | | | | | | | | |
| | | | | | | | | | | |
| | | | | | | | | | | |
| | | | | | | | | | | |
| | | | | | | | | | | |
| | | | | | | | | | | |
| | | | | | | | | | | |
| | | | | | | | | | | |
| | | | | | | | | | | |

Notes:

## Activity     date(s): _____

| | Initials | Time | Bible and Life | Language Arts | Math | World Studies | Science | Arts and Handicraft | Physical Activity | Outings/Life Skill |
|---|---|---|---|---|---|---|---|---|---|---|
| | | | | | | | | | | |
| | | | | | | | | | | |
| | | | | | | | | | | |
| | | | | | | | | | | |
| | | | | | | | | | | |
| | | | | | | | | | | |
| | | | | | | | | | | |
| | | | | | | | | | | |
| | | | | | | | | | | |
| | | | | | | | | | | |
| | | | | | | | | | | |
| | | | | | | | | | | |
| | | | | | | | | | | |

Notes:

# Activity

date(s): _____

| | Initials | Time | Bible and Life | Language Arts | Math | World Studies | Science | Arts and Handicraft | Physical Activity | Outings/Life Skill |
|---|---|---|---|---|---|---|---|---|---|---|
| _____ | | | | | | | | | | |
| _____ | | | | | | | | | | |
| _____ | | | | | | | | | | |
| _____ | | | | | | | | | | |
| _____ | | | | | | | | | | |
| _____ | | | | | | | | | | |
| _____ | | | | | | | | | | |
| _____ | | | | | | | | | | |
| _____ | | | | | | | | | | |
| _____ | | | | | | | | | | |
| _____ | | | | | | | | | | |
| _____ | | | | | | | | | | |
| _____ | | | | | | | | | | |

Notes:

# Activity

date(s): _____

| | Initials | Time | Bible and Life | Language Arts | Math | World Studies | Science | Arts and Handicraft | Physical Activity | Outings/Life Skill |
|---|---|---|---|---|---|---|---|---|---|---|
| | | | | | | | | | | |
| | | | | | | | | | | |
| | | | | | | | | | | |
| | | | | | | | | | | |
| | | | | | | | | | | |
| | | | | | | | | | | |
| | | | | | | | | | | |
| | | | | | | | | | | |
| | | | | | | | | | | |
| | | | | | | | | | | |
| | | | | | | | | | | |
| | | | | | | | | | | |

Notes:

# Activity

date(s): _____

|  | Initials | Time | Bible and Life | Language Arts | Math | World Studies | Science | Arts and Handicraft | Physical Activity | Outings/Life Skiill |
|---|---|---|---|---|---|---|---|---|---|---|
| | | | | | | | | | | |
| | | | | | | | | | | |
| | | | | | | | | | | |
| | | | | | | | | | | |
| | | | | | | | | | | |
| | | | | | | | | | | |
| | | | | | | | | | | |
| | | | | | | | | | | |
| | | | | | | | | | | |
| | | | | | | | | | | |
| | | | | | | | | | | |
| | | | | | | | | | | |
| | | | | | | | | | | |

Notes:

# Activity

date(s): _____

|  | Initials | Time | Bible and Life | Language Arts | Math | World Studies | Science | Arts and Handicraft | Physical Activity | Outings/Life Skill |
|---|---|---|---|---|---|---|---|---|---|---|
| | | | | | | | | | | |
| | | | | | | | | | | |
| | | | | | | | | | | |
| | | | | | | | | | | |
| | | | | | | | | | | |
| | | | | | | | | | | |
| | | | | | | | | | | |
| | | | | | | | | | | |
| | | | | | | | | | | |
| | | | | | | | | | | |
| | | | | | | | | | | |
| | | | | | | | | | | |
| | | | | | | | | | | |

Notes:

# Activity

date(s): _____

| | Initials | Time | Bible and Life | Language Arts | Math | World Studies | Science | Arts and Handicraft | Physical Activity | Outings/Life Skill |
|---|---|---|---|---|---|---|---|---|---|---|
| | | | | | | | | | | |
| | | | | | | | | | | |
| | | | | | | | | | | |
| | | | | | | | | | | |
| | | | | | | | | | | |
| | | | | | | | | | | |
| | | | | | | | | | | |
| | | | | | | | | | | |
| | | | | | | | | | | |
| | | | | | | | | | | |
| | | | | | | | | | | |
| | | | | | | | | | | |
| | | | | | | | | | | |

Notes:

# Activity

date(s): _____

| | Initials | Time | Bible and Life | Language Arts | Math | World Studies | Science | Arts and Handicraft | Physical Activity | Outings/Life Skill |
|---|---|---|---|---|---|---|---|---|---|---|
| | | | | | | | | | | |
| | | | | | | | | | | |
| | | | | | | | | | | |
| | | | | | | | | | | |
| | | | | | | | | | | |
| | | | | | | | | | | |
| | | | | | | | | | | |
| | | | | | | | | | | |
| | | | | | | | | | | |
| | | | | | | | | | | |
| | | | | | | | | | | |
| | | | | | | | | | | |
| | | | | | | | | | | |

Notes:

# Activity

date(s): _____

| | Initials | Time | Bible and Life | Language Arts | Math | World Studies | Science | Arts and Handicraft | Physical Activity | Outings/Life Skill |
|---|---|---|---|---|---|---|---|---|---|---|
| | | | | | | | | | | |
| | | | | | | | | | | |
| | | | | | | | | | | |
| | | | | | | | | | | |
| | | | | | | | | | | |
| | | | | | | | | | | |
| | | | | | | | | | | |
| | | | | | | | | | | |
| | | | | | | | | | | |
| | | | | | | | | | | |
| | | | | | | | | | | |
| | | | | | | | | | | |
| | | | | | | | | | | |

Notes:

# Activity

date(s): _____

| | Initials | Time | Bible and Life | Language Arts | Math | World Studies | Science | Arts and Handicraft | Physical Activity | Outings/Life Skill |
|---|---|---|---|---|---|---|---|---|---|---|
| | | | | | | | | | | |
| | | | | | | | | | | |
| | | | | | | | | | | |
| | | | | | | | | | | |
| | | | | | | | | | | |
| | | | | | | | | | | |
| | | | | | | | | | | |
| | | | | | | | | | | |
| | | | | | | | | | | |
| | | | | | | | | | | |
| | | | | | | | | | | |
| | | | | | | | | | | |
| | | | | | | | | | | |

Notes:

# Activity

date(s): _____

| | Initials | Time | Bible and Life | Language Arts | Math | World Studies | Science | Arts and Handicraft | Physical Activity | Outings/Life Skill |
|---|---|---|---|---|---|---|---|---|---|---|
| | | | | | | | | | | |
| | | | | | | | | | | |
| | | | | | | | | | | |
| | | | | | | | | | | |
| | | | | | | | | | | |
| | | | | | | | | | | |
| | | | | | | | | | | |
| | | | | | | | | | | |
| | | | | | | | | | | |
| | | | | | | | | | | |
| | | | | | | | | | | |
| | | | | | | | | | | |
| | | | | | | | | | | |

Notes:

# Activity

date(s): _____

| | Initials | Time | Bible and Life | Language Arts | Math | World Studies | Science | Arts and Handicraft | Physical Activity | Outings/Life Skill |
|---|---|---|---|---|---|---|---|---|---|---|
| | | | | | | | | | | |
| | | | | | | | | | | |
| | | | | | | | | | | |
| | | | | | | | | | | |
| | | | | | | | | | | |
| | | | | | | | | | | |
| | | | | | | | | | | |
| | | | | | | | | | | |
| | | | | | | | | | | |
| | | | | | | | | | | |
| | | | | | | | | | | |
| | | | | | | | | | | |
| | | | | | | | | | | |

Notes:

# Activity

date(s): _____

| | Initials | Time | Bible and Life | Language Arts | Math | World Studies | Science | Arts and Handicraft | Physical Activity | Outings/Life Skill |
|---|---|---|---|---|---|---|---|---|---|---|
| _____ | | | | | | | | | | |
| _____ | | | | | | | | | | |
| _____ | | | | | | | | | | |
| _____ | | | | | | | | | | |
| _____ | | | | | | | | | | |
| _____ | | | | | | | | | | |
| _____ | | | | | | | | | | |
| _____ | | | | | | | | | | |
| _____ | | | | | | | | | | |
| _____ | | | | | | | | | | |
| _____ | | | | | | | | | | |
| _____ | | | | | | | | | | |

Notes:

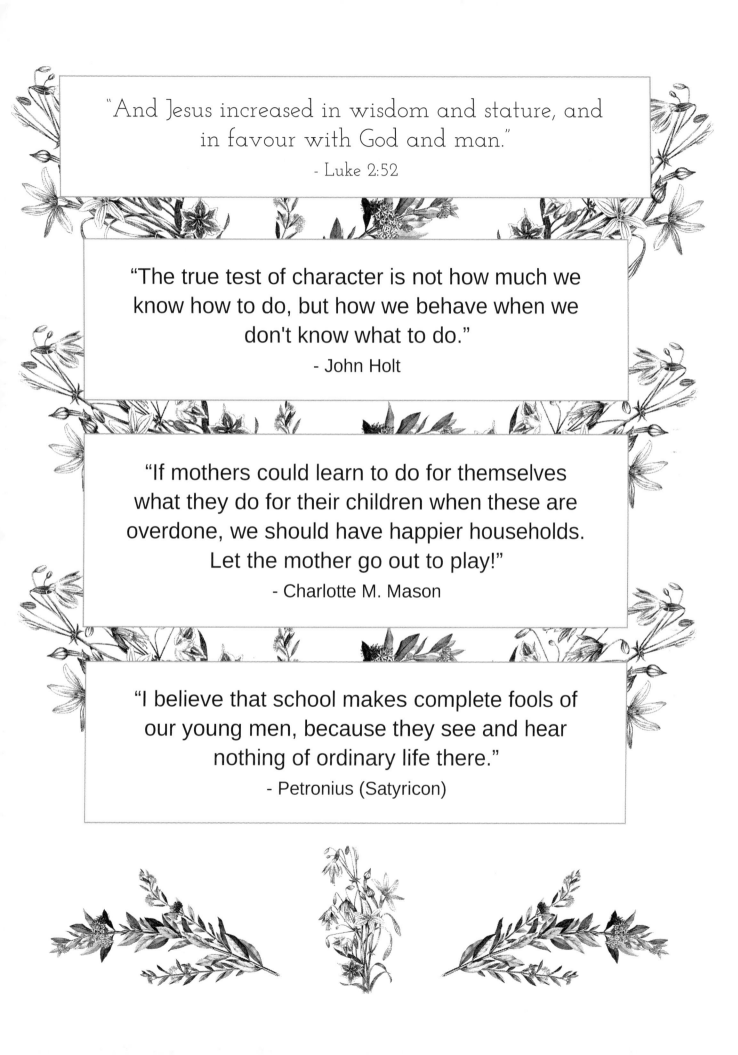

"And Jesus increased in wisdom and stature, and in favour with God and man."
- Luke 2:52

"The true test of character is not how much we know how to do, but how we behave when we don't know what to do."
- John Holt

"If mothers could learn to do for themselves what they do for their children when these are overdone, we should have happier households. Let the mother go out to play!"
- Charlotte M. Mason

"I believe that school makes complete fools of our young men, because they see and hear nothing of ordinary life there."
- Petronius (Satyricon)

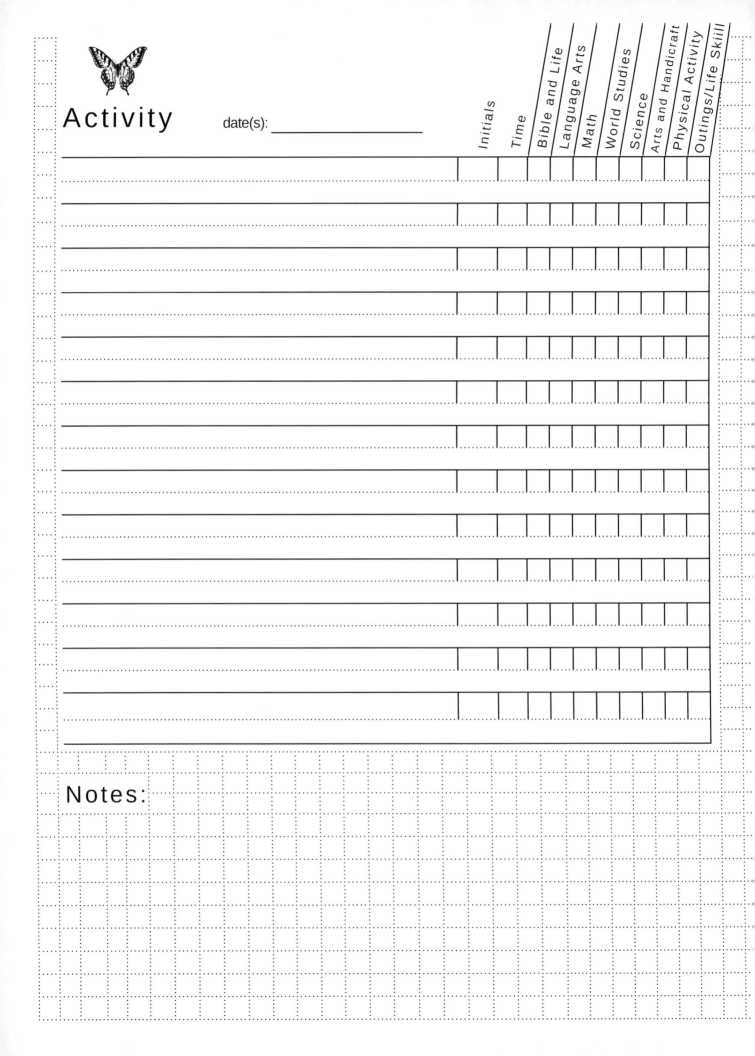

# Activity

date(s): _____

| | Initials | Time | Bible and Life | Language Arts | Math | World Studies | Science | Arts and Handicraft | Physical Activity | Outings/Life Skill |
|---|---|---|---|---|---|---|---|---|---|---|
| _____ | | | | | | | | | | |
| _____ | | | | | | | | | | |
| _____ | | | | | | | | | | |
| _____ | | | | | | | | | | |
| _____ | | | | | | | | | | |
| _____ | | | | | | | | | | |
| _____ | | | | | | | | | | |
| _____ | | | | | | | | | | |
| _____ | | | | | | | | | | |
| _____ | | | | | | | | | | |
| _____ | | | | | | | | | | |
| _____ | | | | | | | | | | |
| _____ | | | | | | | | | | |

Notes:

# Activity

date(s): _____

| | Initials | Time | Bible and Life | Language Arts | Math | World Studies | Science | Arts and Handicraft | Physical Activity | Outings/Life Skiill |
|---|---|---|---|---|---|---|---|---|---|---|
| | | | | | | | | | | |
| | | | | | | | | | | |
| | | | | | | | | | | |
| | | | | | | | | | | |
| | | | | | | | | | | |
| | | | | | | | | | | |
| | | | | | | | | | | |
| | | | | | | | | | | |
| | | | | | | | | | | |
| | | | | | | | | | | |
| | | | | | | | | | | |
| | | | | | | | | | | |
| | | | | | | | | | | |

Notes:

# Activity

date(s): _____

| | Initials | Time | Bible and Life | Language Arts | Math | World Studies | Science | Arts and Handicraft | Physical Activity | Outings/Life Skiill |
|---|---|---|---|---|---|---|---|---|---|---|
| | | | | | | | | | | |
| | | | | | | | | | | |
| | | | | | | | | | | |
| | | | | | | | | | | |
| | | | | | | | | | | |
| | | | | | | | | | | |
| | | | | | | | | | | |
| | | | | | | | | | | |
| | | | | | | | | | | |
| | | | | | | | | | | |
| | | | | | | | | | | |
| | | | | | | | | | | |
| | | | | | | | | | | |

Notes:

# Activity

date(s): _____

| | Initials | Time | Bible and Life | Language Arts | Math | World Studies | Science | Arts and Handicraft | Physical Activity | Outings/Life Skiill |
|---|---|---|---|---|---|---|---|---|---|---|
| | | | | | | | | | | |
| | | | | | | | | | | |
| | | | | | | | | | | |
| | | | | | | | | | | |
| | | | | | | | | | | |
| | | | | | | | | | | |
| | | | | | | | | | | |
| | | | | | | | | | | |
| | | | | | | | | | | |
| | | | | | | | | | | |
| | | | | | | | | | | |
| | | | | | | | | | | |
| | | | | | | | | | | |

Notes:

# Activity

date(s): _____

| | Initials | Time | Bible and Life | Language Arts | Math | World Studies | Science | Arts and Handicraft | Physical Activity | Outings/Life Skill |
|---|---|---|---|---|---|---|---|---|---|---|
| | | | | | | | | | | |
| | | | | | | | | | | |
| | | | | | | | | | | |
| | | | | | | | | | | |
| | | | | | | | | | | |
| | | | | | | | | | | |
| | | | | | | | | | | |
| | | | | | | | | | | |
| | | | | | | | | | | |
| | | | | | | | | | | |
| | | | | | | | | | | |
| | | | | | | | | | | |
| | | | | | | | | | | |

Notes:

# Activity

date(s): _____

| | Initials | Time | Bible and Life | Language Arts | Math | World Studies | Science | Arts and Handicraft | Physical Activity | Outings/Life Skiill |
|---|---|---|---|---|---|---|---|---|---|---|
| | | | | | | | | | | |
| | | | | | | | | | | |
| | | | | | | | | | | |
| | | | | | | | | | | |
| | | | | | | | | | | |
| | | | | | | | | | | |
| | | | | | | | | | | |
| | | | | | | | | | | |
| | | | | | | | | | | |
| | | | | | | | | | | |
| | | | | | | | | | | |
| | | | | | | | | | | |

Notes:

# Activity

date(s): _____

| | Initials | Time | Bible and Life | Language Arts | Math | World Studies | Science | Arts and Handicraft | Physical Activity | Outings/Life Skill |
|---|---|---|---|---|---|---|---|---|---|---|
| | | | | | | | | | | |
| | | | | | | | | | | |
| | | | | | | | | | | |
| | | | | | | | | | | |
| | | | | | | | | | | |
| | | | | | | | | | | |
| | | | | | | | | | | |
| | | | | | | | | | | |
| | | | | | | | | | | |
| | | | | | | | | | | |
| | | | | | | | | | | |
| | | | | | | | | | | |
| | | | | | | | | | | |

Notes:

# Activity

date(s): _____

| | Initials | Time | Bible and Life | Language Arts | Math | World Studies | Science | Arts and Handicraft | Physical Activity | Outings/Life Skill |
|---|---|---|---|---|---|---|---|---|---|---|
| | | | | | | | | | | |
| | | | | | | | | | | |
| | | | | | | | | | | |
| | | | | | | | | | | |
| | | | | | | | | | | |
| | | | | | | | | | | |
| | | | | | | | | | | |
| | | | | | | | | | | |
| | | | | | | | | | | |
| | | | | | | | | | | |
| | | | | | | | | | | |
| | | | | | | | | | | |
| | | | | | | | | | | |

Notes:

# Activity

date(s): _____

|  | Initials | Time | Bible and Life | Language Arts | Math | World Studies | Science | Arts and Handicraft | Physical Activity | Outings/Life Skill |
|---|---|---|---|---|---|---|---|---|---|---|
| _____ |  |  |  |  |  |  |  |  |  |  |
| _____ |  |  |  |  |  |  |  |  |  |  |
| _____ |  |  |  |  |  |  |  |  |  |  |
| _____ |  |  |  |  |  |  |  |  |  |  |
| _____ |  |  |  |  |  |  |  |  |  |  |
| _____ |  |  |  |  |  |  |  |  |  |  |
| _____ |  |  |  |  |  |  |  |  |  |  |
| _____ |  |  |  |  |  |  |  |  |  |  |
| _____ |  |  |  |  |  |  |  |  |  |  |
| _____ |  |  |  |  |  |  |  |  |  |  |
| _____ |  |  |  |  |  |  |  |  |  |  |
| _____ |  |  |  |  |  |  |  |  |  |  |
| _____ |  |  |  |  |  |  |  |  |  |  |

Notes:

# Activity

date(s): _____

| | Initials | Time | Bible and Life | Language Arts | Math | World Studies | Science | Arts and Handicraft | Physical Activity | Outings/Life Skill |
|---|---|---|---|---|---|---|---|---|---|---|
| | | | | | | | | | | |
| | | | | | | | | | | |
| | | | | | | | | | | |
| | | | | | | | | | | |
| | | | | | | | | | | |
| | | | | | | | | | | |
| | | | | | | | | | | |
| | | | | | | | | | | |
| | | | | | | | | | | |
| | | | | | | | | | | |
| | | | | | | | | | | |
| | | | | | | | | | | |
| | | | | | | | | | | |

Notes:

# Activity

date(s): _____

| | Initials | Time | Bible and Life | Language Arts | Math | World Studies | Science | Arts and Handicraft | Physical Activity | Outings/Life Skill |
|---|---|---|---|---|---|---|---|---|---|---|
| | | | | | | | | | | |
| | | | | | | | | | | |
| | | | | | | | | | | |
| | | | | | | | | | | |
| | | | | | | | | | | |
| | | | | | | | | | | |
| | | | | | | | | | | |
| | | | | | | | | | | |
| | | | | | | | | | | |
| | | | | | | | | | | |
| | | | | | | | | | | |
| | | | | | | | | | | |
| | | | | | | | | | | |

Notes:

# Activity

date(s): _____

|  | Initials | Time | Bible and Life | Language Arts | Math | World Studies | Science | Arts and Handicraft | Physical Activity | Outings/Life Skill |
|---|---|---|---|---|---|---|---|---|---|---|
| | | | | | | | | | | |
| | | | | | | | | | | |
| | | | | | | | | | | |
| | | | | | | | | | | |
| | | | | | | | | | | |
| | | | | | | | | | | |
| | | | | | | | | | | |
| | | | | | | | | | | |
| | | | | | | | | | | |
| | | | | | | | | | | |
| | | | | | | | | | | |
| | | | | | | | | | | |

Notes:

# Activity

date(s): _____

| | Initials | Time | Bible and Life | Language Arts | Math | World Studies | Science | Arts and Handicraft | Physical Activity | Outings/Life Skill |
|---|---|---|---|---|---|---|---|---|---|---|
| | | | | | | | | | | |
| | | | | | | | | | | |
| | | | | | | | | | | |
| | | | | | | | | | | |
| | | | | | | | | | | |
| | | | | | | | | | | |
| | | | | | | | | | | |
| | | | | | | | | | | |
| | | | | | | | | | | |
| | | | | | | | | | | |
| | | | | | | | | | | |
| | | | | | | | | | | |
| | | | | | | | | | | |
| | | | | | | | | | | |

Notes:

# Activity

date(s): _____

|  | Initials | Time | Bible and Life | Language Arts | Math | World Studies | Science | Arts and Handicraft | Physical Activity | Outings/Life Skill |
|---|---|---|---|---|---|---|---|---|---|---|
|  |  |  |  |  |  |  |  |  |  |  |
|  |  |  |  |  |  |  |  |  |  |  |
|  |  |  |  |  |  |  |  |  |  |  |
|  |  |  |  |  |  |  |  |  |  |  |
|  |  |  |  |  |  |  |  |  |  |  |
|  |  |  |  |  |  |  |  |  |  |  |
|  |  |  |  |  |  |  |  |  |  |  |
|  |  |  |  |  |  |  |  |  |  |  |
|  |  |  |  |  |  |  |  |  |  |  |
|  |  |  |  |  |  |  |  |  |  |  |
|  |  |  |  |  |  |  |  |  |  |  |
|  |  |  |  |  |  |  |  |  |  |  |
|  |  |  |  |  |  |  |  |  |  |  |

Notes:

# Activity

date(s): _____

| | Initials | Time | Bible and Life | Language Arts | Math | World Studies | Science | Arts and Handicraft | Physical Activity | Outings/Life Skill |
|---|---|---|---|---|---|---|---|---|---|---|
| | | | | | | | | | | |
| | | | | | | | | | | |
| | | | | | | | | | | |
| | | | | | | | | | | |
| | | | | | | | | | | |
| | | | | | | | | | | |
| | | | | | | | | | | |
| | | | | | | | | | | |
| | | | | | | | | | | |
| | | | | | | | | | | |
| | | | | | | | | | | |
| | | | | | | | | | | |
| | | | | | | | | | | |

Notes:

# Activity

date(s): _____

|  | Initials | Time | Bible and Life | Language Arts | Math | World Studies | Science | Arts and Handicraft | Physical Activity | Outings/Life Skiill |
|---|---|---|---|---|---|---|---|---|---|---|
| _____ | | | | | | | | | | |
| _____ | | | | | | | | | | |
| _____ | | | | | | | | | | |
| _____ | | | | | | | | | | |
| _____ | | | | | | | | | | |
| _____ | | | | | | | | | | |
| _____ | | | | | | | | | | |
| _____ | | | | | | | | | | |
| _____ | | | | | | | | | | |
| _____ | | | | | | | | | | |
| _____ | | | | | | | | | | |
| _____ | | | | | | | | | | |
| _____ | | | | | | | | | | |

Notes:

# Activity

date(s): _____

|  | Initials | Time | Bible and Life | Language Arts | Math | World Studies | Science | Arts and Handicraft | Physical Activity | Outings/Life Skiill |
|---|---|---|---|---|---|---|---|---|---|---|
| | | | | | | | | | | |
| | | | | | | | | | | |
| | | | | | | | | | | |
| | | | | | | | | | | |
| | | | | | | | | | | |
| | | | | | | | | | | |
| | | | | | | | | | | |
| | | | | | | | | | | |
| | | | | | | | | | | |
| | | | | | | | | | | |
| | | | | | | | | | | |
| | | | | | | | | | | |
| | | | | | | | | | | |

Notes:

# Activity

date(s): _____

| | Initials | Time | Bible and Life | Language Arts | Math | World Studies | Science | Arts and Handicraft | Physical Activity | Outings/Life Skiill |
|---|---|---|---|---|---|---|---|---|---|---|
| | | | | | | | | | | |
| | | | | | | | | | | |
| | | | | | | | | | | |
| | | | | | | | | | | |
| | | | | | | | | | | |
| | | | | | | | | | | |
| | | | | | | | | | | |
| | | | | | | | | | | |
| | | | | | | | | | | |
| | | | | | | | | | | |
| | | | | | | | | | | |
| | | | | | | | | | | |
| | | | | | | | | | | |

Notes:

# Activity

date(s): _____

| | Initials | Time | Bible and Life | Language Arts | Math | World Studies | Science | Arts and Handicraft | Physical Activity | Outings/Life Skiill |
|---|---|---|---|---|---|---|---|---|---|---|
| _____ | | | | | | | | | | |
| _____ | | | | | | | | | | |
| _____ | | | | | | | | | | |
| _____ | | | | | | | | | | |
| _____ | | | | | | | | | | |
| _____ | | | | | | | | | | |
| _____ | | | | | | | | | | |
| _____ | | | | | | | | | | |
| _____ | | | | | | | | | | |
| _____ | | | | | | | | | | |
| _____ | | | | | | | | | | |
| _____ | | | | | | | | | | |
| _____ | | | | | | | | | | |
| _____ | | | | | | | | | | |

Notes:

# Activity

date(s): _____

| | Initials | Time | Bible and Life | Language Arts | Math | World Studies | Science | Arts and Handicraft | Physical Activity | Outings/Life Skiill |
|---|---|---|---|---|---|---|---|---|---|---|
| | | | | | | | | | | |
| | | | | | | | | | | |
| | | | | | | | | | | |
| | | | | | | | | | | |
| | | | | | | | | | | |
| | | | | | | | | | | |
| | | | | | | | | | | |
| | | | | | | | | | | |
| | | | | | | | | | | |
| | | | | | | | | | | |
| | | | | | | | | | | |
| | | | | | | | | | | |
| | | | | | | | | | | |

Notes:

THE RECORD BOOK • MOMDELIGHTS.COM

# Activity

date(s): _____

| | Initials | Time | Bible and Life | Language Arts | Math | World Studies | Science | Arts and Handicraft | Physical Activity | Outings/Life Skill |
|---|---|---|---|---|---|---|---|---|---|---|
| | | | | | | | | | | |
| | | | | | | | | | | |
| | | | | | | | | | | |
| | | | | | | | | | | |
| | | | | | | | | | | |
| | | | | | | | | | | |
| | | | | | | | | | | |
| | | | | | | | | | | |
| | | | | | | | | | | |
| | | | | | | | | | | |
| | | | | | | | | | | |
| | | | | | | | | | | |
| | | | | | | | | | | |

Notes:

# Activity

date(s): _____

| | Initials | Time | Bible and Life | Language Arts | Math | World Studies | Science | Arts and Handicraft | Physical Activity | Outings/Life Skiill |
|---|---|---|---|---|---|---|---|---|---|---|
| _____ | | | | | | | | | | |
| _____ | | | | | | | | | | |
| _____ | | | | | | | | | | |
| _____ | | | | | | | | | | |
| _____ | | | | | | | | | | |
| _____ | | | | | | | | | | |
| _____ | | | | | | | | | | |
| _____ | | | | | | | | | | |
| _____ | | | | | | | | | | |
| _____ | | | | | | | | | | |
| _____ | | | | | | | | | | |
| _____ | | | | | | | | | | |

Notes:

# Activity

date(s): _____

| | Initials | Time | Bible and Life | Language Arts | Math | World Studies | Science | Arts and Handicraft | Physical Activity | Outings/Life Skill |
|---|---|---|---|---|---|---|---|---|---|---|
| | | | | | | | | | | |
| | | | | | | | | | | |
| | | | | | | | | | | |
| | | | | | | | | | | |
| | | | | | | | | | | |
| | | | | | | | | | | |
| | | | | | | | | | | |
| | | | | | | | | | | |
| | | | | | | | | | | |
| | | | | | | | | | | |
| | | | | | | | | | | |
| | | | | | | | | | | |
| | | | | | | | | | | |

Notes:

# Activity

date(s): _____

|  | Initials | Time | Bible and Life | Language Arts | Math | World Studies | Science | Arts and Handicraft | Physical Activity | Outings/Life Skill |
|---|---|---|---|---|---|---|---|---|---|---|
| | | | | | | | | | | |
| | | | | | | | | | | |
| | | | | | | | | | | |
| | | | | | | | | | | |
| | | | | | | | | | | |
| | | | | | | | | | | |
| | | | | | | | | | | |
| | | | | | | | | | | |
| | | | | | | | | | | |
| | | | | | | | | | | |
| | | | | | | | | | | |
| | | | | | | | | | | |

Notes:

# Activity

date(s): _____

| | Initials | Time | Bible and Life | Language Arts | Math | World Studies | Science | Arts and Handicraft | Physical Activity | Outings/Life Skill |
|---|---|---|---|---|---|---|---|---|---|---|
| | | | | | | | | | | |
| | | | | | | | | | | |
| | | | | | | | | | | |
| | | | | | | | | | | |
| | | | | | | | | | | |
| | | | | | | | | | | |
| | | | | | | | | | | |
| | | | | | | | | | | |
| | | | | | | | | | | |
| | | | | | | | | | | |
| | | | | | | | | | | |
| | | | | | | | | | | |
| | | | | | | | | | | |

Notes:

# Activity

date(s): _____

|  | Initials | Time | Bible and Life | Language Arts | Math | World Studies | Science | Arts and Handicraft | Physical Activity | Outings/Life Skill |
|---|---|---|---|---|---|---|---|---|---|---|
| _____ | | | | | | | | | | |
| _____ | | | | | | | | | | |
| _____ | | | | | | | | | | |
| _____ | | | | | | | | | | |
| _____ | | | | | | | | | | |
| _____ | | | | | | | | | | |
| _____ | | | | | | | | | | |
| _____ | | | | | | | | | | |
| _____ | | | | | | | | | | |
| _____ | | | | | | | | | | |
| _____ | | | | | | | | | | |
| _____ | | | | | | | | | | |
| _____ | | | | | | | | | | |

Notes:

# Activity

date(s): _____

|  | Initials | Time | Bible and Life | Language Arts | Math | World Studies | Science | Arts and Handicraft | Physical Activity | Outings/Life Skill |
|---|---|---|---|---|---|---|---|---|---|---|
| _____ | | | | | | | | | | |
| _____ | | | | | | | | | | |
| _____ | | | | | | | | | | |
| _____ | | | | | | | | | | |
| _____ | | | | | | | | | | |
| _____ | | | | | | | | | | |
| _____ | | | | | | | | | | |
| _____ | | | | | | | | | | |
| _____ | | | | | | | | | | |
| _____ | | | | | | | | | | |
| _____ | | | | | | | | | | |
| _____ | | | | | | | | | | |
| _____ | | | | | | | | | | |

Notes:

# Activity

date(s): _____

| | Initials | Time | Bible and Life | Language Arts | Math | World Studies | Science | Arts and Handicraft | Physical Activity | Outings/Life Skill |
|---|---|---|---|---|---|---|---|---|---|---|
| | | | | | | | | | | |
| | | | | | | | | | | |
| | | | | | | | | | | |
| | | | | | | | | | | |
| | | | | | | | | | | |
| | | | | | | | | | | |
| | | | | | | | | | | |
| | | | | | | | | | | |
| | | | | | | | | | | |
| | | | | | | | | | | |
| | | | | | | | | | | |
| | | | | | | | | | | |
| | | | | | | | | | | |

Notes:

# Activity

date(s): _____

| | Initials | Time | Bible and Life | Language Arts | Math | World Studies | Science | Arts and Handicraft | Physical Activity | Outings/Life Skill |
|---|---|---|---|---|---|---|---|---|---|---|
| | | | | | | | | | | |
| | | | | | | | | | | |
| | | | | | | | | | | |
| | | | | | | | | | | |
| | | | | | | | | | | |
| | | | | | | | | | | |
| | | | | | | | | | | |
| | | | | | | | | | | |
| | | | | | | | | | | |
| | | | | | | | | | | |
| | | | | | | | | | | |
| | | | | | | | | | | |
| | | | | | | | | | | |

Notes:

# Activity

date(s): _____

|  | Initials | Time | Bible and Life | Language Arts | Math | World Studies | Science | Arts and Handicraft | Physical Activity | Outings/Life Skill |
|---|---|---|---|---|---|---|---|---|---|---|
| | | | | | | | | | | |
| | | | | | | | | | | |
| | | | | | | | | | | |
| | | | | | | | | | | |
| | | | | | | | | | | |
| | | | | | | | | | | |
| | | | | | | | | | | |
| | | | | | | | | | | |
| | | | | | | | | | | |
| | | | | | | | | | | |
| | | | | | | | | | | |
| | | | | | | | | | | |
| | | | | | | | | | | |

Notes:

# Activity

date(s): _____

| | Initials | Time | Bible and Life | Language Arts | Math | World Studies | Science | Arts and Handicraft | Physical Activity | Outings/Life Skill |
|---|---|---|---|---|---|---|---|---|---|---|
| | | | | | | | | | | |
| | | | | | | | | | | |
| | | | | | | | | | | |
| | | | | | | | | | | |
| | | | | | | | | | | |
| | | | | | | | | | | |
| | | | | | | | | | | |
| | | | | | | | | | | |
| | | | | | | | | | | |
| | | | | | | | | | | |
| | | | | | | | | | | |
| | | | | | | | | | | |
| | | | | | | | | | | |

Notes:

# Activity

date(s): _____

|  | Initials | Time | Bible and Life | Language Arts | Math | World Studies | Science | Arts and Handicraft | Physical Activity | Outings/Life Skill |
|---|---|---|---|---|---|---|---|---|---|---|
| | | | | | | | | | | |
| | | | | | | | | | | |
| | | | | | | | | | | |
| | | | | | | | | | | |
| | | | | | | | | | | |
| | | | | | | | | | | |
| | | | | | | | | | | |
| | | | | | | | | | | |
| | | | | | | | | | | |
| | | | | | | | | | | |
| | | | | | | | | | | |
| | | | | | | | | | | |
| | | | | | | | | | | |

Notes:

# Activity

date(s): _____

| | Initials | Time | Bible and Life | Language Arts | Math | World Studies | Science | Arts and Handicraft | Physical Activity | Outings/Life Skiill |
|---|---|---|---|---|---|---|---|---|---|---|
| | | | | | | | | | | |
| | | | | | | | | | | |
| | | | | | | | | | | |
| | | | | | | | | | | |
| | | | | | | | | | | |
| | | | | | | | | | | |
| | | | | | | | | | | |
| | | | | | | | | | | |
| | | | | | | | | | | |
| | | | | | | | | | | |
| | | | | | | | | | | |
| | | | | | | | | | | |
| | | | | | | | | | | |

Notes:

# Activity

date(s): _____

| | Initials | Time | Bible and Life | Language Arts | Math | World Studies | Science | Arts and Handicraft | Physical Activity | Outings/Life Skiill |
|---|---|---|---|---|---|---|---|---|---|---|
| _____ | | | | | | | | | | |
| _____ | | | | | | | | | | |
| _____ | | | | | | | | | | |
| _____ | | | | | | | | | | |
| _____ | | | | | | | | | | |
| _____ | | | | | | | | | | |
| _____ | | | | | | | | | | |
| _____ | | | | | | | | | | |
| _____ | | | | | | | | | | |
| _____ | | | | | | | | | | |
| _____ | | | | | | | | | | |
| _____ | | | | | | | | | | |

Notes:

# Activity

date(s): _____

| | Initials | Time | Bible and Life | Language Arts | Math | World Studies | Science | Arts and Handicraft | Physical Activity | Outings/Life Skill |
|---|---|---|---|---|---|---|---|---|---|---|
| | | | | | | | | | | |
| | | | | | | | | | | |
| | | | | | | | | | | |
| | | | | | | | | | | |
| | | | | | | | | | | |
| | | | | | | | | | | |
| | | | | | | | | | | |
| | | | | | | | | | | |
| | | | | | | | | | | |
| | | | | | | | | | | |
| | | | | | | | | | | |
| | | | | | | | | | | |
| | | | | | | | | | | |

Notes:

# Activity

date(s): _____

| | Initials | Time | Bible and Life | Language Arts | Math | World Studies | Science | Arts and Handicraft | Physical Activity | Outings/Life Skill |
|---|---|---|---|---|---|---|---|---|---|---|
| | | | | | | | | | | |
| | | | | | | | | | | |
| | | | | | | | | | | |
| | | | | | | | | | | |
| | | | | | | | | | | |
| | | | | | | | | | | |
| | | | | | | | | | | |
| | | | | | | | | | | |
| | | | | | | | | | | |
| | | | | | | | | | | |
| | | | | | | | | | | |
| | | | | | | | | | | |
| | | | | | | | | | | |

Notes:

"Every good gift and every perfect gift is from above, and cometh down from the Father of lights, with whom is no variableness, neither shadow of turning."
- James 1:17

"The true picture of the effective home teacher is more often a secure and happy mom."
- Dr. Raymond Moore, *The Successful Homeschool Family Handbook*

"We certainly do not value creativity as a way to save the world. We value it because God put creativity into a person and we value the person."
- Ruth Beechick, *From Heart and Mind: What the Bible Says About Learning*

"I learned most, not from those who taught me but from those who talked with me."
- St. Augustine

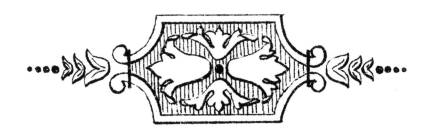

# Activity

date(s): _____

| | Initials | Time | Bible and Life | Language Arts | Math | World Studies | Science | Arts and Handicraft | Physical Activity | Outings/Life Skill |
|---|---|---|---|---|---|---|---|---|---|---|
| | | | | | | | | | | |
| | | | | | | | | | | |
| | | | | | | | | | | |
| | | | | | | | | | | |
| | | | | | | | | | | |
| | | | | | | | | | | |
| | | | | | | | | | | |
| | | | | | | | | | | |
| | | | | | | | | | | |
| | | | | | | | | | | |
| | | | | | | | | | | |
| | | | | | | | | | | |
| | | | | | | | | | | |

Notes:

# Activity

date(s): _____

| | Initials | Time | Bible and Life | Language Arts | Math | World Studies | Science | Arts and Handicraft | Physical Activity | Outings/Life Skill |
|---|---|---|---|---|---|---|---|---|---|---|
| | | | | | | | | | | |
| | | | | | | | | | | |
| | | | | | | | | | | |
| | | | | | | | | | | |
| | | | | | | | | | | |
| | | | | | | | | | | |
| | | | | | | | | | | |
| | | | | | | | | | | |
| | | | | | | | | | | |
| | | | | | | | | | | |
| | | | | | | | | | | |
| | | | | | | | | | | |
| | | | | | | | | | | |

Notes:

# Activity

date(s): _____

| | Initials | Time | Bible and Life | Language Arts | Math | World Studies | Science | Arts and Handicraft | Physical Activity | Outings/Life Skill |
|---|---|---|---|---|---|---|---|---|---|---|
| | | | | | | | | | | |
| | | | | | | | | | | |
| | | | | | | | | | | |
| | | | | | | | | | | |
| | | | | | | | | | | |
| | | | | | | | | | | |
| | | | | | | | | | | |
| | | | | | | | | | | |
| | | | | | | | | | | |
| | | | | | | | | | | |
| | | | | | | | | | | |
| | | | | | | | | | | |

Notes:

# Activity

date(s): _____

|  | Initials | Time | Bible and Life | Language Arts | Math | World Studies | Science | Arts and Handicraft | Physical Activity | Outings/Life Skill |
|---|---|---|---|---|---|---|---|---|---|---|
| | | | | | | | | | | |
| | | | | | | | | | | |
| | | | | | | | | | | |
| | | | | | | | | | | |
| | | | | | | | | | | |
| | | | | | | | | | | |
| | | | | | | | | | | |
| | | | | | | | | | | |
| | | | | | | | | | | |
| | | | | | | | | | | |
| | | | | | | | | | | |
| | | | | | | | | | | |
| | | | | | | | | | | |

Notes:

# Activity

date(s): _____

|  | Initials | Time | Bible and Life | Language Arts | Math | World Studies | Science | Arts and Handicraft | Physical Activity | Outings/Life Skill |
|---|---|---|---|---|---|---|---|---|---|---|
| | | | | | | | | | | |
| | | | | | | | | | | |
| | | | | | | | | | | |
| | | | | | | | | | | |
| | | | | | | | | | | |
| | | | | | | | | | | |
| | | | | | | | | | | |
| | | | | | | | | | | |
| | | | | | | | | | | |
| | | | | | | | | | | |
| | | | | | | | | | | |
| | | | | | | | | | | |
| | | | | | | | | | | |

Notes:

# Activity

date(s): _____

| | Initials | Time | Bible and Life | Language Arts | Math | World Studies | Science | Arts and Handicraft | Physical Activity | Outings/Life Skill |
|---|---|---|---|---|---|---|---|---|---|---|
| | | | | | | | | | | |
| | | | | | | | | | | |
| | | | | | | | | | | |
| | | | | | | | | | | |
| | | | | | | | | | | |
| | | | | | | | | | | |
| | | | | | | | | | | |
| | | | | | | | | | | |
| | | | | | | | | | | |
| | | | | | | | | | | |
| | | | | | | | | | | |
| | | | | | | | | | | |
| | | | | | | | | | | |

Notes:

# Activity

date(s): _____

| | Initials | Time | Bible and Life | Language Arts | Math | World Studies | Science | Arts and Handicraft | Physical Activity | Outings/Life Skill |
|---|---|---|---|---|---|---|---|---|---|---|
| | | | | | | | | | | |
| | | | | | | | | | | |
| | | | | | | | | | | |
| | | | | | | | | | | |
| | | | | | | | | | | |
| | | | | | | | | | | |
| | | | | | | | | | | |
| | | | | | | | | | | |
| | | | | | | | | | | |
| | | | | | | | | | | |
| | | | | | | | | | | |
| | | | | | | | | | | |

Notes:

# Activity

date(s): _____

| | Initials | Time | Bible and Life | Language Arts | Math | World Studies | Science | Arts and Handicraft | Physical Activity | Outings/Life Skiill |
|---|---|---|---|---|---|---|---|---|---|---|
| | | | | | | | | | | |
| | | | | | | | | | | |
| | | | | | | | | | | |
| | | | | | | | | | | |
| | | | | | | | | | | |
| | | | | | | | | | | |
| | | | | | | | | | | |
| | | | | | | | | | | |
| | | | | | | | | | | |
| | | | | | | | | | | |
| | | | | | | | | | | |
| | | | | | | | | | | |
| | | | | | | | | | | |

Notes:

# Activity

date(s): _____

| | Initials | Time | Bible and Life | Language Arts | Math | World Studies | Science | Arts and Handicraft | Physical Activity | Outings/Life Skill |
|---|---|---|---|---|---|---|---|---|---|---|
| | | | | | | | | | | |
| | | | | | | | | | | |
| | | | | | | | | | | |
| | | | | | | | | | | |
| | | | | | | | | | | |
| | | | | | | | | | | |
| | | | | | | | | | | |
| | | | | | | | | | | |
| | | | | | | | | | | |
| | | | | | | | | | | |
| | | | | | | | | | | |
| | | | | | | | | | | |
| | | | | | | | | | | |

Notes:

# Activity

date(s): _____

|  | Initials | Time | Bible and Life | Language Arts | Math | World Studies | Science | Arts and Handicraft | Physical Activity | Outings/Life Skill |
|---|---|---|---|---|---|---|---|---|---|---|
| ............................................ | | | | | | | | | | |
| ............................................ | | | | | | | | | | |
| ............................................ | | | | | | | | | | |
| ............................................ | | | | | | | | | | |
| ............................................ | | | | | | | | | | |
| ............................................ | | | | | | | | | | |
| ............................................ | | | | | | | | | | |
| ............................................ | | | | | | | | | | |
| ............................................ | | | | | | | | | | |
| ............................................ | | | | | | | | | | |
| ............................................ | | | | | | | | | | |
| ............................................ | | | | | | | | | | |
| ............................................ | | | | | | | | | | |

Notes:

# Activity

date(s): _____

| | Initials | Time | Bible and Life | Language Arts | Math | World Studies | Science | Arts and Handicraft | Physical Activity | Outings/Life Skill |
|---|---|---|---|---|---|---|---|---|---|---|
| | | | | | | | | | | |
| | | | | | | | | | | |
| | | | | | | | | | | |
| | | | | | | | | | | |
| | | | | | | | | | | |
| | | | | | | | | | | |
| | | | | | | | | | | |
| | | | | | | | | | | |
| | | | | | | | | | | |
| | | | | | | | | | | |
| | | | | | | | | | | |
| | | | | | | | | | | |
| | | | | | | | | | | |

Notes:

THE RECORD BOOK • MOMDELIGHTS.COM

# Activity

date(s): _____

| | Initials | Time | Bible and Life | Language Arts | Math | World Studies | Science | Arts and Handicraft | Physical Activity | Outings/Life Skill |
|---|---|---|---|---|---|---|---|---|---|---|
| | | | | | | | | | | |
| | | | | | | | | | | |
| | | | | | | | | | | |
| | | | | | | | | | | |
| | | | | | | | | | | |
| | | | | | | | | | | |
| | | | | | | | | | | |
| | | | | | | | | | | |
| | | | | | | | | | | |
| | | | | | | | | | | |
| | | | | | | | | | | |
| | | | | | | | | | | |
| | | | | | | | | | | |

Notes:

# Activity

date(s): _____

| | Initials | Time | Bible and Life | Language Arts | Math | World Studies | Science | Arts and Handicraft | Physical Activity | Outings/Life Skiill |
|---|---|---|---|---|---|---|---|---|---|---|
| | | | | | | | | | | |
| | | | | | | | | | | |
| | | | | | | | | | | |
| | | | | | | | | | | |
| | | | | | | | | | | |
| | | | | | | | | | | |
| | | | | | | | | | | |
| | | | | | | | | | | |
| | | | | | | | | | | |
| | | | | | | | | | | |
| | | | | | | | | | | |
| | | | | | | | | | | |
| | | | | | | | | | | |

Notes:

# Activity

date(s): _____

| | Initials | Time | Bible and Life | Language Arts | Math | World Studies | Science | Arts and Handicraft | Physical Activity | Outings/Life Skill |
|---|---|---|---|---|---|---|---|---|---|---|
| | | | | | | | | | | |
| | | | | | | | | | | |
| | | | | | | | | | | |
| | | | | | | | | | | |
| | | | | | | | | | | |
| | | | | | | | | | | |
| | | | | | | | | | | |
| | | | | | | | | | | |
| | | | | | | | | | | |
| | | | | | | | | | | |
| | | | | | | | | | | |
| | | | | | | | | | | |
| | | | | | | | | | | |

Notes:

# Activity

date(s): _____

| | Initials | Time | Bible and Life | Language Arts | Math | World Studies | Science | Arts and Handicraft | Physical Activity | Outings/Life Skill |
|---|---|---|---|---|---|---|---|---|---|---|
| | | | | | | | | | | |
| | | | | | | | | | | |
| | | | | | | | | | | |
| | | | | | | | | | | |
| | | | | | | | | | | |
| | | | | | | | | | | |
| | | | | | | | | | | |
| | | | | | | | | | | |
| | | | | | | | | | | |
| | | | | | | | | | | |
| | | | | | | | | | | |
| | | | | | | | | | | |
| | | | | | | | | | | |
| | | | | | | | | | | |

Notes:

# Activity

date(s): _____

| | Initials | Time | Bible and Life | Language Arts | Math | World Studies | Science | Arts and Handicraft | Physical Activity | Outings/Life Skill |
|---|---|---|---|---|---|---|---|---|---|---|
| | | | | | | | | | | |
| | | | | | | | | | | |
| | | | | | | | | | | |
| | | | | | | | | | | |
| | | | | | | | | | | |
| | | | | | | | | | | |
| | | | | | | | | | | |
| | | | | | | | | | | |
| | | | | | | | | | | |
| | | | | | | | | | | |
| | | | | | | | | | | |
| | | | | | | | | | | |
| | | | | | | | | | | |

Notes:

# Activity

date(s): _____

| | Initials | Time | Bible and Life | Language Arts | Math | World Studies | Science | Arts and Handicraft | Physical Activity | Outings/Life Skiill |
|---|---|---|---|---|---|---|---|---|---|---|
| | | | | | | | | | | |
| | | | | | | | | | | |
| | | | | | | | | | | |
| | | | | | | | | | | |
| | | | | | | | | | | |
| | | | | | | | | | | |
| | | | | | | | | | | |
| | | | | | | | | | | |
| | | | | | | | | | | |
| | | | | | | | | | | |
| | | | | | | | | | | |
| | | | | | | | | | | |
| | | | | | | | | | | |

Notes:

# Activity

date(s): _____

| | Initials | Time | Bible and Life | Language Arts | Math | World Studies | Science | Arts and Handicraft | Physical Activity | Outings/Life Skill |
|---|---|---|---|---|---|---|---|---|---|---|
| | | | | | | | | | | |
| | | | | | | | | | | |
| | | | | | | | | | | |
| | | | | | | | | | | |
| | | | | | | | | | | |
| | | | | | | | | | | |
| | | | | | | | | | | |
| | | | | | | | | | | |
| | | | | | | | | | | |
| | | | | | | | | | | |
| | | | | | | | | | | |
| | | | | | | | | | | |
| | | | | | | | | | | |

Notes:

# Activity

date(s): _____

| | Initials | Time | Bible and Life | Language Arts | Math | World Studies | Science | Arts and Handicraft | Physical Activity | Outings/Life Skill |
|---|---|---|---|---|---|---|---|---|---|---|
| | | | | | | | | | | |
| | | | | | | | | | | |
| | | | | | | | | | | |
| | | | | | | | | | | |
| | | | | | | | | | | |
| | | | | | | | | | | |
| | | | | | | | | | | |
| | | | | | | | | | | |
| | | | | | | | | | | |
| | | | | | | | | | | |
| | | | | | | | | | | |
| | | | | | | | | | | |

Notes:

# Activity

date(s): _____

|  | Initials | Time | Bible and Life | Language Arts | Math | World Studies | Science | Arts and Handicraft | Physical Activity | Outings/Life Skill |
|---|---|---|---|---|---|---|---|---|---|---|
| | | | | | | | | | | |
| | | | | | | | | | | |
| | | | | | | | | | | |
| | | | | | | | | | | |
| | | | | | | | | | | |
| | | | | | | | | | | |
| | | | | | | | | | | |
| | | | | | | | | | | |
| | | | | | | | | | | |
| | | | | | | | | | | |
| | | | | | | | | | | |
| | | | | | | | | | | |
| | | | | | | | | | | |

Notes:

# Activity

date(s): _____

| | Initials | Time | Bible and Life | Language Arts | Math | World Studies | Science | Arts and Handicraft | Physical Activity | Outings/Life Skill |
|---|---|---|---|---|---|---|---|---|---|---|
| | | | | | | | | | | |
| | | | | | | | | | | |
| | | | | | | | | | | |
| | | | | | | | | | | |
| | | | | | | | | | | |
| | | | | | | | | | | |
| | | | | | | | | | | |
| | | | | | | | | | | |
| | | | | | | | | | | |
| | | | | | | | | | | |
| | | | | | | | | | | |
| | | | | | | | | | | |
| | | | | | | | | | | |

Notes:

# Activity

date(s): _____

|  | Initials | Time | Bible and Life | Language Arts | Math | World Studies | Science | Arts and Handicraft | Physical Activity | Outings/Life Skill |
|---|---|---|---|---|---|---|---|---|---|---|
| | | | | | | | | | | |
| | | | | | | | | | | |
| | | | | | | | | | | |
| | | | | | | | | | | |
| | | | | | | | | | | |
| | | | | | | | | | | |
| | | | | | | | | | | |
| | | | | | | | | | | |
| | | | | | | | | | | |
| | | | | | | | | | | |
| | | | | | | | | | | |
| | | | | | | | | | | |
| | | | | | | | | | | |

Notes:

# Activity

date(s): _____

| | Initials | Time | Bible and Life | Language Arts | Math | World Studies | Science | Arts and Handicraft | Physical Activity | Outings/Life Skiill |
|---|---|---|---|---|---|---|---|---|---|---|
| | | | | | | | | | | |
| | | | | | | | | | | |
| | | | | | | | | | | |
| | | | | | | | | | | |
| | | | | | | | | | | |
| | | | | | | | | | | |
| | | | | | | | | | | |
| | | | | | | | | | | |
| | | | | | | | | | | |
| | | | | | | | | | | |
| | | | | | | | | | | |
| | | | | | | | | | | |
| | | | | | | | | | | |

Notes:

# Activity

date(s): _____

| | Initials | Time | Bible and Life | Language Arts | Math | World Studies | Science | Arts and Handicraft | Physical Activity | Outings/Life Skiill |
|---|---|---|---|---|---|---|---|---|---|---|
| | | | | | | | | | | |
| | | | | | | | | | | |
| | | | | | | | | | | |
| | | | | | | | | | | |
| | | | | | | | | | | |
| | | | | | | | | | | |
| | | | | | | | | | | |
| | | | | | | | | | | |
| | | | | | | | | | | |
| | | | | | | | | | | |
| | | | | | | | | | | |
| | | | | | | | | | | |
| | | | | | | | | | | |

Notes:

# Activity

date(s): _____

| | Initials | Time | Bible and Life | Language Arts | Math | World Studies | Science | Arts and Handicraft | Physical Activity | Outings/Life Skill |
|---|---|---|---|---|---|---|---|---|---|---|
| _____ | | | | | | | | | | |
| _____ | | | | | | | | | | |
| _____ | | | | | | | | | | |
| _____ | | | | | | | | | | |
| _____ | | | | | | | | | | |
| _____ | | | | | | | | | | |
| _____ | | | | | | | | | | |
| _____ | | | | | | | | | | |
| _____ | | | | | | | | | | |
| _____ | | | | | | | | | | |
| _____ | | | | | | | | | | |
| _____ | | | | | | | | | | |
| _____ | | | | | | | | | | |

Notes:

THE RECORD BOOK • MOMDELIGHTS.COM

## Activity

date(s): _____

| | Initials | Time | Bible and Life | Language Arts | Math | World Studies | Science | Arts and Handicraft | Physical Activity | Outings/Life Skiill |
|---|---|---|---|---|---|---|---|---|---|---|
| _____ | | | | | | | | | | |
| _____ | | | | | | | | | | |
| _____ | | | | | | | | | | |
| _____ | | | | | | | | | | |
| _____ | | | | | | | | | | |
| _____ | | | | | | | | | | |
| _____ | | | | | | | | | | |
| _____ | | | | | | | | | | |
| _____ | | | | | | | | | | |
| _____ | | | | | | | | | | |
| _____ | | | | | | | | | | |
| _____ | | | | | | | | | | |
| _____ | | | | | | | | | | |

Notes:

# Activity

date(s): _____

|  | Initials | Time | Bible and Life | Language Arts | Math | World Studies | Science | Arts and Handicraft | Physical Activity | Outings/Life Skill |
|---|---|---|---|---|---|---|---|---|---|---|
| _____ |  |  |  |  |  |  |  |  |  |  |
| _____ |  |  |  |  |  |  |  |  |  |  |
| _____ |  |  |  |  |  |  |  |  |  |  |
| _____ |  |  |  |  |  |  |  |  |  |  |
| _____ |  |  |  |  |  |  |  |  |  |  |
| _____ |  |  |  |  |  |  |  |  |  |  |
| _____ |  |  |  |  |  |  |  |  |  |  |
| _____ |  |  |  |  |  |  |  |  |  |  |
| _____ |  |  |  |  |  |  |  |  |  |  |
| _____ |  |  |  |  |  |  |  |  |  |  |
| _____ |  |  |  |  |  |  |  |  |  |  |
| _____ |  |  |  |  |  |  |  |  |  |  |

Notes:

# Activity

date(s): _____

| | Initials | Time | Bible and Life | Language Arts | Math | World Studies | Science | Arts and Handicraft | Physical Activity | Outings/Life Skill |
|---|---|---|---|---|---|---|---|---|---|---|
| | | | | | | | | | | |
| | | | | | | | | | | |
| | | | | | | | | | | |
| | | | | | | | | | | |
| | | | | | | | | | | |
| | | | | | | | | | | |
| | | | | | | | | | | |
| | | | | | | | | | | |
| | | | | | | | | | | |
| | | | | | | | | | | |
| | | | | | | | | | | |
| | | | | | | | | | | |
| | | | | | | | | | | |

Notes:

# Activity

date(s): _____

| | Initials | Time | Bible and Life | Language Arts | Math | World Studies | Science | Arts and Handicraft | Physical Activity | Outings/Life Skiill |
|---|---|---|---|---|---|---|---|---|---|---|
| | | | | | | | | | | |
| | | | | | | | | | | |
| | | | | | | | | | | |
| | | | | | | | | | | |
| | | | | | | | | | | |
| | | | | | | | | | | |
| | | | | | | | | | | |
| | | | | | | | | | | |
| | | | | | | | | | | |
| | | | | | | | | | | |
| | | | | | | | | | | |
| | | | | | | | | | | |
| | | | | | | | | | | |

Notes:

# Activity

date(s): _____

| | Initials | Time | Bible and Life | Language Arts | Math | World Studies | Science | Arts and Handicraft | Physical Activity | Outings/Life Skill |
|---|---|---|---|---|---|---|---|---|---|---|
| | | | | | | | | | | |
| | | | | | | | | | | |
| | | | | | | | | | | |
| | | | | | | | | | | |
| | | | | | | | | | | |
| | | | | | | | | | | |
| | | | | | | | | | | |
| | | | | | | | | | | |
| | | | | | | | | | | |
| | | | | | | | | | | |
| | | | | | | | | | | |
| | | | | | | | | | | |
| | | | | | | | | | | |

Notes:

# Activity

date(s): _____

| | Initials | Time | Bible and Life | Language Arts | Math | World Studies | Science | Arts and Handicraft | Physical Activity | Outings/Life Skiill |
|---|---|---|---|---|---|---|---|---|---|---|
| | | | | | | | | | | |
| | | | | | | | | | | |
| | | | | | | | | | | |
| | | | | | | | | | | |
| | | | | | | | | | | |
| | | | | | | | | | | |
| | | | | | | | | | | |
| | | | | | | | | | | |
| | | | | | | | | | | |
| | | | | | | | | | | |
| | | | | | | | | | | |
| | | | | | | | | | | |

Notes:

# Activity

date(s): _____

| | Initials | Time | Bible and Life | Language Arts | Math | World Studies | Science | Arts and Handicraft | Physical Activity | Outings/Life Skiill |
|---|---|---|---|---|---|---|---|---|---|---|
| | | | | | | | | | | |
| | | | | | | | | | | |
| | | | | | | | | | | |
| | | | | | | | | | | |
| | | | | | | | | | | |
| | | | | | | | | | | |
| | | | | | | | | | | |
| | | | | | | | | | | |
| | | | | | | | | | | |
| | | | | | | | | | | |
| | | | | | | | | | | |
| | | | | | | | | | | |

Notes:

# Activity

date(s): _____

| | Initials | Time | Bible and Life | Language Arts | Math | World Studies | Science | Arts and Handicraft | Physical Activity | Outings/Life Skiill |
|---|---|---|---|---|---|---|---|---|---|---|
| | | | | | | | | | | |
| | | | | | | | | | | |
| | | | | | | | | | | |
| | | | | | | | | | | |
| | | | | | | | | | | |
| | | | | | | | | | | |
| | | | | | | | | | | |
| | | | | | | | | | | |
| | | | | | | | | | | |
| | | | | | | | | | | |
| | | | | | | | | | | |
| | | | | | | | | | | |
| | | | | | | | | | | |

Notes:

# Activity

date(s): _____

| | Initials | Time | Bible and Life | Language Arts | Math | World Studies | Science | Arts and Handicraft | Physical Activity | Outings/Life Skill |
|---|---|---|---|---|---|---|---|---|---|---|
| | | | | | | | | | | |
| | | | | | | | | | | |
| | | | | | | | | | | |
| | | | | | | | | | | |
| | | | | | | | | | | |
| | | | | | | | | | | |
| | | | | | | | | | | |
| | | | | | | | | | | |
| | | | | | | | | | | |
| | | | | | | | | | | |
| | | | | | | | | | | |
| | | | | | | | | | | |
| | | | | | | | | | | |

Notes:

# Activity

date(s): _____

| | Initials | Time | Bible and Life | Language Arts | Math | World Studies | Science | Arts and Handicraft | Physical Activity | Outings/Life Skill |
|---|---|---|---|---|---|---|---|---|---|---|
| | | | | | | | | | | |
| | | | | | | | | | | |
| | | | | | | | | | | |
| | | | | | | | | | | |
| | | | | | | | | | | |
| | | | | | | | | | | |
| | | | | | | | | | | |
| | | | | | | | | | | |
| | | | | | | | | | | |
| | | | | | | | | | | |
| | | | | | | | | | | |
| | | | | | | | | | | |
| | | | | | | | | | | |

Notes:

# Activity

date(s): _____

| | Initials | Time | Bible and Life | Language Arts | Math | World Studies | Science | Arts and Handicraft | Physical Activity | Outings/Life Skill |
|---|---|---|---|---|---|---|---|---|---|---|
| | | | | | | | | | | |
| | | | | | | | | | | |
| | | | | | | | | | | |
| | | | | | | | | | | |
| | | | | | | | | | | |
| | | | | | | | | | | |
| | | | | | | | | | | |
| | | | | | | | | | | |
| | | | | | | | | | | |
| | | | | | | | | | | |
| | | | | | | | | | | |
| | | | | | | | | | | |
| | | | | | | | | | | |

Notes:

# Activity

date(s): _____

| | Initials | Time | Bible and Life | Language Arts | Math | World Studies | Science | Arts and Handicraft | Physical Activity | Outings/Life Skill |
|---|---|---|---|---|---|---|---|---|---|---|

Notes:

Made in United States
Troutdale, OR
09/20/2024

22986413R00117